# CONTEMPORARY'S

# *GED*

# LANGUAGE ARTS, WRITING EXERCISE BOOK

 **Wright Group**

**Editor:** Jennifer Krasula
**Executive Editor:** Linda Kwil
**Creative Director:** Michael E. Kelly
**Marketing Manager:** Sean Klunder
**Production Manager:** Genevieve Kelley
**Manager of Editorial Services:** Sylvia Bace

Interior Design by Think Design Group LLC

 **Wright Group**

Send all inquiries to:
Wright Group/McGraw-Hill
130 E. Randolph, Suite 400
Chicago, IL 60681

ISBN 0-8092-2233-7

7 8 9 10 QDP 08 07

# Table of Contents

# Introduction

*Contemporary's GED Language Arts, Writing Exercise Book* will help you study for both the multiple-choice and essay portions of the GED Language Arts, Writing Test. There are two main parts in this exercise book: **Editing** and **The Essay**. Each part is divided into smaller sections that give you additional practice in the areas covered in *Contemporary's GED Language Arts, Writing* and in the Language Arts, Writing portion of *Contemporary's Complete GED*. The page numbers at the beginning of each section in the exercise book will refer you to the appropriate pages in either text.

This exercise book also contains a full-length **Practice Test.** This test is very similar in length and format to the actual GED Language Arts, Writing Test.

## Overview of the GED Language Arts, Writing Test

The GED Language Arts, Writing Test consists of two parts. Part I: Editing contains 50 multiple-choice questions that are taken from the following content areas:

- Organization (15%)

- Sentence Structure (30%)

- Usage (30%)

- Mechanics (25%)

Some questions will ask you to locate errors in paragraph organization, sentence structure, grammar, punctuation, and spelling. Others may ask you to restate an idea in different words.

In Part II: The Essay, you will be asked to write a well-developed essay presenting an opinion or an explanation of a familiar topic. You should plan and organize your ideas before you write, and revise and edit your essay when you are finished.

## Item Types

Part I of the GED Language Arts, Writing Test consists of item sets. Each item set begins with an informational or business-related document that may contain errors in organization, sentence structure, usage, and mechanics. In the questions following each document, you'll be asked to correct the errors. In Part I of this exercise book, you'll find the GED-type item sets in the exercises marked "GED Practice."

There are three types of questions in these item sets—sentence correction, sentence revision, and construction shift. The following items are examples of each type:

### Sentence Correction Items (45 percent of the questions)

**Sentence 1: Mr. Anderson, why does all the files need to be printed now?**

What correction should be made to sentence 1?

(1) remove the comma after *Anderson*
(2) change *does* to *do*
(3) insert a comma after *files*
(4) change *need* to *needed*
(5) no correction is necessary

As you can see, several different types of errors are suggested in the answer choices. You have to decide whether there is an error in organization, sentence structure, usage, or mechanics, or no error at all. Sometimes the fifth option, *no correction is necessary,* will be the correct answer. Not all items, however, will have that option. The correct answer for this item is choice (2).

### Sentence Revision Items (35 percent of the questions)

**Sentence 2: Several improvements have been made to <u>our office, it's a</u> more pleasant place to work.**

Which is the best way to write the underlined portion of the text? If the original is the best way, choose option (1).

(1) our office, it's a
(2) our office it's a
(3) our office, but it's a
(4) our office, in fact it's a
(5) our office, so it's a

With this type of item, you have to focus on only one part of the sentence—the underlined part. The first answer choice is always the same as the original sentence; the other four choices give you alternative versions. You choose option (1) if the original sentence is correct as written. In this item, the correct answer is choice (5).

**Construction Shift Items (20 percent of the questions)**
In these items, the sentences are not incorrect. Instead of asking you to correct errors, these items ask you to combine or rewrite sentences.

> **Sentence 3: We left the house so that we would be on time for the conference, but we arrived late for the conference.**

If you rewrote sentence 3 beginning with

*Although we left the house,*

The next words should be

(1) on time for the conference, but we
(2) we arrived late for the conference
(3) so that we would be on time, but we arrived
(4) on time, we arrived late for
(5) on time for the conference, we arrived late for the conference

To answer this item, you need to rewrite the sentence in your head. Your goal is to preserve the meaning of the original sentence. If you don't see the correct answer right away, try each answer choice in turn to see which one makes sense. The correct answer in this item is choice (4).

## The Writing Process

Part II of the GED Language Arts, Writing Test consists of a single essay topic that will ask you to respond to a question or an informative statement by using your personal observations, experience, and knowledge. You will only have 45 minutes to write a well-developed essay on the topic, so it is essential that you develop a plan for writing.

The sections in Part II of this exercise book will give you extra practice in the following areas:

- Using a simple four-step writing process

- Writing a five-paragraph essay

- Understanding the requirements of the GED Essay Scoring Guide

At the end of the book is a complete **Answer Key** that tells you the reasoning behind the answers to all the exercises. Be sure to check your answers and to read the explanations. This will help you improve your skills in answering multiple-choice questions and writing essays.

To determine whether or not you are ready to take the real GED Language Arts, Writing Test, we recommend that you take the **Practice Test** at the end of this book. The evaluation chart that follows the test will help you determine the areas in which you may need additional practice.

# Sentence Basics

*Language Arts, Writing pages 19–49*
*Complete GED pages 65–104*

## Sentences versus Sentence Fragments

A **complete sentence** must meet three requirements:

1. It must have a subject that tells *what* or *whom* the sentence is about.

2. It must have a predicate that tells what the subject *is* or *does*.

3. It must express a complete thought.

A group of words that does not pass these three tests is called a **fragment**.

**Fragment:** Last month's check for the rent.

**Sentence:** Last month's check for the rent was mailed today.

**EXERCISE 1**

Part A    **Directions:** In the space provided, write an *F* if the group of words is a fragment or an *S* if it is a sentence. If you write an *F*, tell whether the fragment is missing a subject, predicate, or complete thought.

_____ 1. Time with your family.

_____ 2. Bought groceries and left them on the bus.

_____ 3. This situation calls for some serious attention.

_____ 4. The city council will need seven new members.

_____ 5. Growing wild in the highway median.

Part B    **Directions:** Underline the fragments in the following paragraphs. Then on a separate sheet of paper, rewrite the paragraphs, eliminating all fragments by adding words or combining fragments and sentences.

All employees should arrive at the meeting before nine o'clock tomorrow morning. Important to be on time because we have a lot of issues to discuss. Please be sure to tell your supervisor. If you know you are going to be late.

Most of the meeting will be focused on the new regulations on workers' compensation. Thought it would be wise to provide adequate information about this extremely complex issue.

*Answers are on page 124.*

# Identifying the Simple Subject and Verb

The **simple subject** of a sentence is the key word that tells *what* or *whom* the sentence is about. The **verb** is the part of the predicate that tells what the subject *is* or *does*.

The employee's progress **<u>report</u>** from last month **<u>did seem</u>** fair.
SIMPLE SUBJECT                  VERB

Remember that sometimes the subject comes after the verb in a sentence.

On the top of my to-do list **<u>is</u>** a long **<u>letter</u>** to my landlord.
VERB      SIMPLE SUBJECT

Also remember that a simple subject or verb may be **compound**, or consist of two nouns or two verbs joined by *and*.

**<u>Bruce and Tom plan</u>** to travel to France this spring.
SIMPLE SUBJECT     VERB

The polite **<u>audience sat and listened</u>** to the speech.
SIMPLE SUBJECT     VERB

## EXERCISE 2

**Directions:** Underline and label the simple subject and verb in each sentence.

1. The woman behind the counter will help you immediately.

2. Singing in the choir provides some stress relief for her.

3. In the store window will be a sign announcing our annual sale.

4. The members of the garden club plant roses every year.

5. We wanted to be wary of potential dangers.

6. Supervisors and workers will be asked to complete a survey.

7. All authorized signatures are listed at the end of the document.

8. Three hundred people marched in today's Walk for Peace.

9. Underneath this enthusiasm lies a layer of doubt.

10. Chaperoning one field trip is required of every parent.

11. Those hardworking waiters deserve some time off!

12. More discussion followed after this morning's meeting.

**Answers are on page 124.**

# Commands, Questions, and *Here* or *There* Statements

Finding the simple subject and verb in some sentences can be tricky.

**Command:**   Please <u>bring</u> your application with you to the interview.
   VERB (UNDERSTOOD SUBJECT: YOU)

**Question:**   When <u>will</u> our <u>paychecks</u> <u>arrive</u> at the office?
   VERB            SIMPLE SUBJECT     VERB

**Here/There:**   There <u>were</u> many different <u>ways</u> to look at the problem.
   VERB                           SIMPLE SUBJECT

## EXERCISE 3

**Directions:**   Underline and label the simple subject and verb in each sentence.

1. Where did you put the reports from last Friday's sales?

2. Do not begin the program until approximately 11:00 this morning.

3. Immediately reject any outrageous proposals from this group.

4. Here are the reasons for my son's absences this month.

5. Why did the workers walk off the job?

6. Earlier in the day there were about 75 customers waiting.

7. Did the police officer arrive promptly at the accident scene?

8. There seems to be some serious confusion about your plans.

9. Ms. Bakaar, speak loudly into the microphone.

10. When will the game begin?

11. Will everyone please sit down and listen?

12. Who will be the next person to arrive?

*Answers are on page 124.*

# Plural and Possessive Nouns

A **noun** is a word that labels a person, place, thing, or idea. The nouns in the sentence below are in **boldface.**

The **time** has come for **people** to give their **opinions** about our **government.**

A **plural noun** names more than one person, place, thing, or idea.

one street   ⟶   two **streets**
one story   ⟶   more **stories**
one child   ⟶   lots of **children**

A **possessive noun** is a noun that shows ownership. Possession is shown by adding *'s* to a singular noun and *'* to a plural noun.

the name that belongs to the street   =   the **street's** name
the plot of the story   =   the **story's** plot
the bone that belongs to the dogs   =   the **dogs'** bone

## EXERCISE 4

**Directions:** Each sentence below contains one error in either a possessive or a plural noun. Underline the noun with the error and write the correct noun in the space provided.

1. That mans idea of fun is watching football games all day long. _____

2. All of the story's in this week's magazine are sad and depressing. _____

3. Please read this bulletin about womens rights and tell me what you think. _____

4. One hundred worker's pension plans were reinstated when the computer error was

    discovered. _____

5. We are sorry to inform you that your families application for a rent controlled apartment has

    been denied. _____

6. These documents indicate that your bill was paid in full three month's ago. _____

7. Your sons' left eye was damaged in his recent soccer accident. _____

8. The date for filing your tax's is given in this form's fine print. _____

9. To access your account online, please type in your name and your parents name.

    _____

10. We are delighted to announce that all employee's of this firm will receive full benefits this year.

    _____

*Answers are on page 124.*

# Choosing the Correct Pronoun

The following chart summarizes basic pronoun forms

| SUBJECT | OBJECT | POSSESSIVE | |
|---|---|---|---|
| I | me | my | mine |
| you | you | your | yours |
| he | him | his | his |
| she | her | her | hers |
| it | it | its | its |
| we | us | our | ours |
| they | them | their | theirs |
| who | whom | whose | whose |

**EXERCISE 5**

Part A     **Directions:**    Write a correct pronoun in each blank below. There is more than one correct answer for most sentences.

1. You should notify _____ of your decision as soon as possible.

2. _____ is an outstanding choice for the next chair of the committee.

3. When will you bring _____ children to the office so we can meet them?

4. There are several steps _____ needs to take to secure a loan.

5. We agreed to do this job to the best of _____ ability.

6. _____ books are these?

Part B     **Directions:**    Underline the pronoun error in each sentence below and write the correct form in the space provided.

1. The car you are sitting in happens to be our's. _____

2. Give the files to she so that they can be evaluated. _____

3. The original idea was your, so you should get the credit. _____

4. This job training program will give they a good start. _____

*Answers are on page 124.*

# Pronouns in Compounds

Remember to look at each word in a compound separately to decide what pronoun to use.

**Correct:**    Please be sure to give the report to Ms. Ortega and **me.**

**Incorrect:**    Please be sure to give the report to Ms. Ortega and **I.**

## EXERCISE 6

<u>Part A</u>      **Directions:**    Underline the correct pronoun in each sentence below.

1. The television report shows that the chairman and *(she, her)* are a fine team.

2. Either Mai-Lin or *(him, he)* will be able to answer your questions.

3. Every week I ask Mary and *(they, them)* to stop by my office to chat.

4. *(He, Him)* and my supervisor get along very well.

5. When my wife and *(I, me)* are angry with each other, we seldom yell.

6. A new car was something John and *(they, them)* have wanted for a long time.

7. The manager asked Theresa and *(I, me)* to get to work earlier this week.

8. Giselly and *(him, he)* make a great teaching team this year.

9. Please be sure to sign the form and give it to Howard or *(I, me)*.

10. It looks like the bonus this month will go to *(she, her)* or *(I, me)*.

<u>Part B</u>      **Directions:**    Correct the pronoun errors in the memo below.

TO:     Ms. Ting
FROM:   James Breason
DATE:   December 10, 2001

The staff and me would like to let you know that we are unhappy with your new lateness policy. You ideas about improving performance are good, but the methods you plan to use are not fair to we.

You should not punish people the first time them are late. Instead, maybe you should send a report to the supervisor or hers assistant. Then, if an employee is late again, you could tell he or she that he or she is on probation.

Please tell your boss, Mr. Wayne, to trust your employees to make they own decisions about arrival at work. If you and him punish too quickly, people may begin not to trust you or he.

*Answers are on page 124.*

# Sentence Basics

**Directions:** Choose the <u>one best answer</u> to each question. Some of the sentences may contain errors. A few sentences, however, may be correct as written. Read the sentences carefully and then answer the questions based on them. For each question, choose the answer that would result in the most effective writing of the sentence or sentences.

*Questions 1–8 refer to the following informative brochure.*

## Tips for Improving Your Memory

### (A)

(1) As people age, they begin to lose parts of the brain function that we call memory. (2) Sometimes this memory loss is a simple inconvenience; other times it can signal the beginning of a persons Alzheimer's disease. (3) Scientists are discovering that steps we can take to preserve mental faculties like memory for as long as possible.

### (B)

(4) One tip is to exercise your mind in different ways. (5) Reading, doing crossword puzzles, and taking in new information regularly are all way's to keep those brain synapses firing. (6) Some people even use their skills to take up a new foreign language or sign up for a computer class at they local community college. (7) Even having long conversations with interesting friends or acquaintances is a good strategy for keeping you mind working.

### (C)

(8) Another tip toward memory improvement is to make associations when acquiring new information. (9) In other words, using facts that you already know to remember new facts. (10) For example, if you want to be sure you remember your daughter's new phone number, think about where else in her life some of that number pattern might appear. (11) Perhaps the last digits are 1978, and that also happens to be the year you and her traveled to Florida together. (12) Linking old information to new information strengthens your ability to recall both facts. (13) Why not try some of these idea's and see what happens?

1. Sentence 2: **Sometimes this memory loss is a simple inconvenience; other times it can signal the beginning of a persons Alzheimer's disease.**

   What correction should be made to sentence 2?

   (1) change *Sometimes* to *Sometime's*
   (2) change *it* to *its*
   (3) change *persons* to *persons'*
   (4) change *persons* to *person's*
   (5) no correction is necessary

2. Sentence 3: **Scientists are discovering <u>that steps we can take</u> to preserve mental faculties like memory for as long as possible.**

   Which is the best way to write the underlined portion of the text? If the original is the best way, choose option (1).

   (1) that steps we can take
   (2) that step's we can take
   (3) that steps' we can take
   (4) that there are steps we can take
   (5) that there are step's we can take

3. **Sentence 5: Reading, doing crossword puzzles, and taking in new information regularly are all way's to keep those brain synapses firing.**

   What correction should be made to sentence 5?

   (1) change *puzzles* to *puzzle's*
   (2) change *way's* to *ways*
   (3) change *ways* to *ways'*
   (4) change *synapses* to *synapse's*
   (5) change *those* to *them*

4. **Sentence 6: Some people even use their skills to take up a new foreign language or sign up for a computer class at they local community college.**

   What correction should be made to sentence 6?

   (1) change *their* to *they*
   (2) change *their* to *them*
   (3) change *skills* to *skill's*
   (4) change *they* to *their*
   (5) no correction is necessary

5. **Sentence 7: Even having long conversations with interesting friends or acquaintances is a good strategy for keeping you mind working.**

   What correction should be made to sentence 7?

   (1) change *friends* to *friend's*
   (2) change *acquaintances* to *acquaintances'*
   (3) change *you* to *your*
   (4) change *you* to *yours*
   (5) change *you* to *yours'*

6. **Sentence 9: <u>In other words, using facts that you</u> already know to remember new facts.**

   Which is the best way to write the underlined portion of the text? If the original is the best way, choose option (1).

   (1) In other words, using facts that you
   (2) In other word's, using facts that you
   (3) In other words, use facts that you
   (4) In other words, using fact's that you
   (5) In other words, using facts that your

7. **Sentence 11: Perhaps the last digits are 1978, and that also happens to be the year you and her traveled to Florida together.**

   What correction should be made to sentence 11?

   (1) change *digits* to *digit's*
   (2) change *you* to *your*
   (3) change *her* to *hers*
   (4) change *her* to *she*
   (5) no correction is necessary

8. **Sentence 13: Why not try some of these <u>idea's and see what happens?</u>**

   Which is the best way to write the underlined portion of the text? If the original is the best way, choose option (1).

   (1) idea's and see what happens?
   (2) ideas' and see what happens?
   (3) ideas and see it happens?
   (4) ideas and see him happens?
   (5) ideas and see what happens?

   ***Answers are on page 125.***

Go to **www.GEDWriting.com** for additional practice and instruction!

**PART I, EDITING**

# Using Verbs

Language Arts, Writing pages 51–82
Complete GED pages 73–91

## Simple and Continuing Tenses

Verb tenses are used to show the time when something happens. The examples below show the **simple present, past,** and **future tenses.** They also show examples of the **continuing tenses,** which are used for action that is ongoing in the present, past, or future.

**Present:** Mrs. Muldaur **organizes** social functions. She **is organizing** a function for the president's office.

**Past:** The clerk **mailed** the package yesterday. He **was mailing** it because it was needed in Pittsburgh.

**Future:** I **will think** about your idea. I **will be thinking** about what you said at our meeting.

### EXERCISE 1

**Directions:** Complete each sentence by writing the correct form of the verb in the blank. Use either a simple tense or a continuing tense. More than one answer may be correct in some sentences.

1. *(save)* The technical department usually _____ all documents on disk for at least one year.

2. *(graduate)* We are pleased to inform you that your son _____ from West High School next month with the rest of his class.

3. *(think)* At our last meeting, Mr. Andrews, you said you _____ we could come to some agreement.

4. *(be)* By this evening, 1,700 crates _____ on their way to Japan.

5. *(work)* Your supervisor would like to know when you _____ next week.

6. *(call)* Please let us know the exact time you _____ yesterday.

7. *(go)* When _____ you _____ on vacation this summer?

8. *(take)* My father _____ his lunch to work every day.

9. *(see)* While the nurse runs some tests, you _____ the doctor.

10. *(plant)* We _____ the carrot seeds in the same place every year.

*Answers are on page 125.*

9

# Perfect Tenses

The **perfect tenses** show action completed before a specified time in the past or continuing until a specified time in the future.

**Present Perfect:** We **have asked** for a meeting with the landlord.

**Past Perfect:** As of last week, we **had asked** a total of eight times.

**Future Perfect:** By next Monday, we **will have asked** our last time!

## EXERCISE 2

**Directions:** Complete each sentence below by writing the correct perfect tense in the blank. Use time clues to help you choose the correct tense.

1. *(fire)* By the time you read this memo, Mr. Stevens _____ half of the staff.

2. *(sell)* Over the past several years BestCo _____ more appliances than any other store of its kind.

3. *(borrow)* You and your husband _____ the maximum amount allowed on your credit card.

4. *(build)* By the year 2000 this contractor _____ 25 low-income homes in this city.

5. *(review)* Fortunately the committee _____ your plans and would like to offer you its full support.

6. *(learn)* Every staff member at Smile Daycare Center _____ infant and child CPR.

7. *(restore)* We hope that by 2010 we _____ most of the run-down historic buildings in the county.

8. *(promise)* Before his speech was over last night, the candidate _____ more than he could possibly deliver to his constituents.

9. *(claim)* Repeatedly she _____ that she was treated unfairly by the police officers on duty.

10. *(input)* Over the course of the last three nights Vera _____ every single piece of information into the computer.

*Answers are on page 125.*

# Irregular Verbs

Verbs that are **irregular** do not follow a familiar pattern. The only way to learn the tenses of irregular verbs is to memorize them.

**Incorrect:**    My tutor **comed** to our session on time for once yesterday.

**Correct:**    My tutor **came** to our session on time for once yesterday.

**Incorrect:**    We have **seed** the movie before.

**Correct:**    We have **seen** the movie before.

**EXERCISE 3**

<u>Part A</u>    **Directions:**    Circle the correct verb in each sentence below.

1. Roberto and Mary (*goed, have goed, have gone*) out for three months.

2. The assistant (*brung, brought, bringed*) extra copies of the architect's plans.

3. When the car swerved to the right, the pedestrian (*be, was, been*) hit and killed instantly.

4. By the time the factory closed, every employee (*finded, done find, had found*) a job elsewhere.

5. It was easy to see that Ms. Wu (*runned, had run, had ran*) a festival before.

6. Throughout his years in elementary school, Jack (*been, be, was*) a favorite among the teachers.

7. When Maggie first opened her eyes, the sun already (*raised, had risen, had rose*).

8. Though she was only 11, Anna (*won, winned, had winned*) first place in the swimming competition.

9. The counselor asked who (*seed, had seen, has saw*) the safety video.

10. In the space below please explain any criminal convictions you (*haved, have had, done had*) in the last 24 months.

<u>Part B</u>    **Directions:**    Correct the verb errors in the document below.

### Weekly Report Procedures

1. Record in the logbook any problems you seen during any shift.

2. Be specific about what time the incident taked place and who been involved.

3. Ask your shift partner to verify what you have recorded.

4. When you have did all of the above, sign your report and place it in your supervisor's mailbox.

*Answers are on page 125.*

# Using Consistent Verb Tenses

In a paragraph or longer piece of writing it is important not to switch verb tenses unnecessarily. Some of the questions on Part I of the Language Arts, Writing Test will ask you to make sure that verb tense is consistent in a piece of writing.

## EXERCISE 4

**Directions:** Two incorrect verb tenses are used in each paragraph below. Circle each error and write the correct form above it.

1.    A federal survey published yesterday announced that the rate of violent crime in the United States fell for the sixth year in a row. The Bureau of Justice Statistics said that the number of rapes, assaults, and robberies was reduced by 15 percent during the year 2000. In addition, the report stated, property crimes will fall by 10 percent during the last year. However, critics of the survey stated that these statistics will apply only to reported crime and that many violent crimes are not reported each year.

2.    The following guidelines are designed to help you find the information you need to receive unemployment benefits.

    a.  If you are under age 21, you need to call 1-800-555-1212 and ask for Form 27A.

    b.  If you are over age 65, you needed to report to the Senior Services Department at 123 North Street and show your ID and social security information.

    c.  All other applicants reported to Employment Services, also at 123 North Street.

3.    Here are just some of the benefits you will receive if you open a Customer One account with us today. You had received free checking for six months if you maintain a minimum balance of just $500. You will have the opportunity to do all your banking online with our easy new BankLink program. In addition, you were able to take advantage of our low-interest loans with no money down. Sign up now and receive a free phone card worth $25!

4.    Before you sign any contract or agreement with a home improvement company, make sure you know what you got in return for your money. Unfortunately there are many unlicensed con artists out there who are very skilled at duping unsuspecting consumers. For example, last year one such con man signed up 300 customers for new heating systems that the homes did not even need. By the time the trick was discovered, the criminal "home improvement specialist" will be long gone.

*Answers are on page 125.*

# Subject-Verb Agreement

Choosing a present-tense verb to match a singular or plural subject is called **subject-verb agreement.**

**Incorrect:**    I **works** from 11:00 A.M. until 7:00 P.M. every day.

**Correct:**    I **work** from 11:00 A.M. until 7:00 P.M. every day.

**EXERCISE 5**

<u>Part A</u>    **Directions:**    Underline the correct verb form in each sentence below.

1. You *(wasn't, weren't)* there when I called you last night.

2. This answer *(don't, doesn't)* seem accurate to me at all.

3. When they *(tell, tells)* the truth, things *(is, are)* easier to handle.

4. Every day this week, employees *(bike, bikes)* to work to promote the clean air bill.

5. We *(is, are)* planning to make the announcement at the dinner event tomorrow evening.

6. Many people *(think, thinks)* that our streets *(is, are)* not plowed often enough.

7. Jorge's assistant *(seem, seems)* to have excellent organizational skills.

8. The agreement *(state, states)* that I *(is, am)* able to cancel my order at any time for any reason.

9. Harry's plan *(is, are)* to vacation without interruption.

10. Whatever you *(does, do)*, you usually *(is, are)* successful.

<u>Part B</u>    **Directions:**    Find and correct the errors in subject-verb agreement in the letter below.

January 3, 2002

Dear Customer Service Representative:

I be writing to inquire about an order I placed on November 1 of last year.  The order number are #213980, and it was for a box of 12 votive candles.  The candles is part of the Serenity Collection.

Although I have waited the suggested four weeks for delivery, I still does not have my order.  This do not seem right.  Will you please check on my order and let me know when I can expect delivery?

Your company has always provided me with excellent products and service.  I looks forward to doing more business with you in the future.

Sincerely,

Helen Kim

*Answers are on page 126.*

# Compound Subjects

Deciding what verb form to use with a compound subject can be tricky. Here are the basic rules for determining whether a subject is plural or singular and what verb to use.

- If a compound subject is formed using *and*, the subject is plural. Use a verb that agrees with a plural subject.

   The doctor and Katie **hike** around the pond every day.

- If a compound subject is formed using *or* or *nor*, the verb should agree with the subject closer to it.

   Either Miguel or his brothers **do** the laundry on Sundays.

   Either his brothers or Miguel **does** the laundry on Sundays.

## EXERCISE 6

<u>Part A</u>　　**Directions:**　Underline the correct verb in each sentence below.

1. My brother and sister *(plan, plans)* to get together a week from next Friday.

2. The supervisors and staff *(is, are)* some of the most highly paid professionals in this industry.

3. Either you or I *(am, are)* going to have to complete the project so that we can move forward.

4. You and the person next to the exit *(needs, need)* to be able to get out quickly.

5. Neither the cat nor the dogs *(has, have)* been fed yet today.

6. Maria and the Sullivans usually *(has, have)* their annual barbecue picnic for the staff of Renewal House.

7. We think that either Taneesha or you *(is, are)* the best person to write up a list of guidelines for the group.

8. The clean-up crew and the janitor *(doesn't, don't)* work late on a day like this.

9. Prescription drugs and alcohol *(is, are)* the most abused substances in this country today.

10. When someone moves, either bits of trash or old furniture *(is, are)* usually left behind.

<u>Part B</u>     **Directions:**     Find and correct the subject-verb agreement errors in the letter below.

February 2, 2002

Ms. Nancy Kensington
Director of Personnel
Fashion Designers, Inc.
900 Fourth Avenue
Newton, MA 02458

Dear Ms. Kensington:

I called your office yesterday, and your secretary suggested that I write you a letter and enclose my résumé. She believe you are planning to do some hiring over the next several months, and I am very interested in working for your company.

My experience in clothing have been widespread as you will see from my enclosed résumé.  I worked for several years in a tailor's shop, mending and altering both men's and women's clothing. And for the past two years, both my day job and my evening job shows me that my future is in fashion.  During the day I be involved in matching customers with attractive styles at Dresses and More in the mall. At night I work at Style Plus Factory inspecting fabrics.  Both these current jobs and my past experience is a good indication of my skills and interests.

I am looking forward to hearing from you soon, Ms. Kensington.  As for my references, either my current employers or Mr. Chang are available at the phone numbers listed on my résumé.

Thank you for your time.

Sincerely,

Crystal Collier

*Answers are on page 126.*

# Inverted Word Order

Subject-verb agreement can be tricky when the verb precedes the subject in a sentence or when the subject is understood, as in a command. Changing the order of the words in the sentence can help.

Why **(does, do)** the time go so slowly in the afternoon?

becomes

The time **does go** so slowly in the afternoon.

**EXERCISE 7**

Part A    **Directions:**    Circle the subject and underline the correct verb in each sentence below.

1. When *(do, does)* the cook usually serve breakfast in the morning?

2. Ellen, please *(tell, tells)* the truth to the best of your ability.

3. There *(is, are)* many explanations for this outcome if we are open-minded.

4. The nurses are wondering why there *(is, are)* never a doctor on the psychiatric ward between noon and one o'clock.

5. Why *(does, do)* we have to call the main office in order to speak to a customer service representative?

6. *(Was, Were)* there enough forms to go around?

7. Reverend Riley, please *(come, comes)* to dinner around six o'clock next Monday night.

8. *(Does, Do)* these chairs need to be rearranged for the meeting, or *(is, are)* the room set up correctly?

9. Here *(sit, sits)* the most wonderful colleagues I could ever have.

10. There *(go, goes)* an old friend of mine from high school.

Part B    **Directions:**    Find and correct the errors in subject-verb agreement in the article below.

A company spokesperson are expected to announce today that Castle Camera Company plans to lay off 100 more workers within the next month. This figure represents approximately one-quarter of the company's entire workforce. Neither employees nor company president Maureen Burns were available for comment.

Castle Camera, founded in 1925, are a major employer in this region, and the job loss is considered a major blow to the local economy. "There are no silver lining in this announcement," said Mayor Esther Hauser.

*Answers are on page 127.*

# Prepositional Phrases and Other Interrupters

Sometimes a subject is separated from its verb by a prepositional phrase or another group of words. When this is the case, be especially careful that the subject and verb agree.

**Incorrect:** The files on his desk **is** covered with coffee.

**Correct:** The files on his desk **are** covered with coffee.

**EXERCISE 8**

<u>Part A</u>    **Directions:**  Choose the correct verb in each sentence below.

1. The customers in line *(looks, look)* tired and frustrated.

2. There is a rumor that your daughter, along with another teenager, *(was, were)* caught stealing from a store in the mall.

3. The woman carrying all those books *(is, are)* the new librarian in the city branch.

4. Flexibility, in addition to commitment, *(seem, seems)* to be a key ingredient in a successful marriage.

5. Fortunately the children in that car *(has, have)* seat belts on.

6. This parking lot, like all the others, *(is, are)* reserved for commuters with valid stickers.

7. Please make sure that the personal files on his computer *(is, are)* removed immediately.

8. The time for announcements *(has, have)* finally arrived.

9. Our wishes for a speedy recovery *(is, are)* included.

10. Your supervisor, together with her director, *(think, thinks)* you deserve a pay raise and a new title.

<u>Part B</u>    **Directions:**  Find and correct the subject-verb agreement errors in the letter below.

March 1, 2002

Dear Isabel,

I'm writing just to tell you that I, along with Joanna, misses working with you at Coffee Plus. Your bright smile and cheerful personality is sorely needed around here. In addition, the work you used to do in transcriptions were first rate, and no one can take your place!

Do you enjoy your new office? I know your decision to leave the people here were difficult. But you probably have lots of new friends and an easier pace and climate in which to work. I heard that three other people in your office is also former Coffee Plus employees!

Best,

Bev

*Answers are on page 127.*

# Indefinite Pronouns

Sometimes it is difficult to figure out whether an **indefinite pronoun** is singular or plural. Here are some examples:

| | |
|---|---|
| **Singular:** | each, neither, either, nothing, nobody, no one, everyone, everything, someone, something, anyone, anything |
| **Plural:** | both, few, many, several |
| **Singular or plural:** | some, most, any, none, all |

The indefinite pronouns in the last category can be either singular or plural, depending on how they are used in a sentence.

**Some** of the report has been **typed.**

**Some** of my answers **have been changed.**

## EXERCISE 9

**Directions:**   Circle the indefinite pronoun and underline the correct verb in each sentence below.

1. Either of the two top salespeople *(is, are)* going to the district meeting in Florida this year.

2. Most of our friends *(appears, appear)* younger than 50 because they exercise and live healthful lives.

3. All of the pieces of cake *(was, were)* eaten before the last customers came in.

4. We knew that all of the casserole *(was, were)* already cleared away.

5. Several in this group *(do, does)* volunteer work at the local soup kitchen.

6. Lisa says that nothing in these documents *(looks, look)* out of order.

7. Please understand that anyone living in these apartments *(receive, receives)* a statement at the end of the year.

8. Of all my ideas, why *(does, do)* so few make it to the weekly agenda?

9. The suspect knew that anything she said *(was, were)* permitted as evidence in a court of law.

10. Everything we were looking for that day *(was, were)* found at the discount mall on Route 47.

11. Once the meeting has started, everyone *(get, gets)* equal opportunity to speak about the new policies.

12. Both of the brothers *(walk, walks)* with a slight limp.

13. The factory foreman said that no one *(go, goes)* on break until the whistle has blown.

14. Some of my thoughts *(is, are)* personal.

15. Some of this music *(is, are)* great.

*Answers are on page 127.*

# Using Verbs

**Directions:** Choose the <u>one best answer</u> to each question. Some of the sentences may contain errors. A few sentences, however, may be correct as written. Read the sentences carefully and then answer the questions based on them. For each question, choose the answer that would result in the most effective writing of the sentence or sentences.

*Questions 1 –9 refer to the following memo.*

TO:     All Nexent Employees

FROM: Sam Bain, Director of Health and Safety

(1) This memo is sent to remind you of proper safety procedures both on the factory floor and in the cafeteria.  (2) It has come to my attention that the policies stated in our handbook is not being followed in many instances.  (3) Here is the basic rules and regulations:

- (4) All areas of Building A has been designated "Hard hat required."  (5) This means that you may not enter this building BY ANY ENTRANCE without a company-approved head covering.  (6) If either you or a coworker need access to this building, please get the proper gear from the warehouse.

- (7) Inside all buildings the floor space inside the painted yellow lines are considered "live."  (8) In other words, anyone inside these lines must have a specific reason for being there and must be completing a specific task.  (9) Absolutely no loitering or socializing are allowed in live space.

- (10) Please remember that electricity on all lines runs day and night.  (11) Use caution when washing down floors at the end of your shift.

- (12) There are no eating or drinking ANYWHERE inside the buildings except in the cafeteria.

- (13) Before your lunch shift and before all breaks, your hands should be thoroughly cleaned. (14) Grease from the machinery, in addition to chemical residues from the dyes, are dangerous if ingested.

- (15) The health and safety consultant for all shifts are now Margaret Kingsbury; please see her if you have any specific questions or comments.

(16) If everyone works together on these issues, we will all have a safe and productive work environment.

1. **Sentence 2: It has come to my attention that the policies stated in our handbook <u>is not being followed</u> in many instances.**

   Which is the best way to write the underlined portion of the text? If the original is the best way, choose option (1).

   (1)  is not being followed
   (2)  was not being followed
   (3)  are not being followed
   (4)  is not been followed
   (5)  is not being follow

2. **Sentence 3: Here is the basic rules and regulations:**

   What correction should be made to sentence 3?

   (1)  change *Here* to *There*
   (2)  change *is* to *was*
   (3)  change *is* to *are*
   (4)  change *rules* to *rule's*
   (5)  change *regulations* to *regulation's*

3. Sentence 4: **All areas of Building A <u>has been designated</u> "Hard hat required."**

   Which is the best way to write the underlined portion of the text?  If the original is the best way, choose option (1).

   (1)  has been designated
   (2)  have been designated
   (3)  been designated
   (4)  is designated
   (5)  was designated

4. Sentence 6: **If either you or a coworker need access to this building, please get the proper gear from the warehouse.**

   What correction should be made to sentence 6?

   (1)  change *you* to *your*
   (2)  change *you* to *he*
   (3)  change *need* to *needed*
   (4)  change *need* to *needs*
   (5)  change *get* to *gets*

5. Sentence 7: **Inside all buildings the floor space inside the painted yellow lines <u>are considered</u> "live."**

   Which is the best way to write the underlined portion of the text?  If the original is the best way, choose option (1).

   (1)  are considered
   (2)  were considered
   (3)  were considering
   (4)  consider
   (5)  is considered

6. Sentence 9: **Absolutely no loitering or socializing are allowed in live space.**

   What correction should be made to sentence 9?

   (1)  change *are* to *is*
   (2)  change *are* to *was*
   (3)  change *are* to *were*
   (4)  change *allowed* to *allow*
   (5)  no correction is necessary

7. Sentence 12: **There are no eating or drinking ANYWHERE inside the buildings except in the cafeteria.**

   What correction should be made to sentence 12?

   (1)  change *There* to *There's*
   (2)  change *are* to *is*
   (3)  change *are* to *were*
   (4)  change *are* to *be*
   (5)  no correction is necessary

8. Sentence 14: **Grease from the machinery, in addition to chemical <u>residues from the dyes, are</u> dangerous if ingested.**

   Which is the best way to write the underlined portion of the text?  If the original is the best way, choose option (1).

   (1)  residues from the dyes, are
   (2)  residues from the dye's, are
   (3)  residue's from the dyes, are
   (4)  residues from the dyes, is
   (5)  residues from the dyes, being

9. Sentence 15: **The health and safety consultant for all <u>shifts are now</u> Margaret Kingsbury; please see her if you have any specific questions or comments.**

   Which is the best way to write the underlined portion of the text? If the original is the best way, choose option (1).

   (1)  shifts are now
   (2)  shift's are now
   (3)  shifts is now
   (4)  shifts being now
   (5)  shifts be now

   *Answers are on page 127.*

# Cumulative Review

**Directions:** Choose the <u>one best answer</u> to each question. Some of the sentences may contain errors in organization, sentence structure, usage, and mechanics. A few sentences, however, may be correct as written. Read the sentences carefully and then answer the questions based on them. For each question, choose the answer that would result in the most effective writing of the sentence or sentences.

*Questions 1–6 refer to the following safety brochure.*

## Cellular Phone Safety Warning

### (A)

(1) We are pleased that you have selected PortoPhone for you cellular phone needs. (2) For people on the go, a portable phone has become an essential tool for keeping in contact in both their personal and professional live's. (3) While we believe in the importance of this form of communication, there is also some potential dangers that we are obligated to discuss with you. (4) These dangers primarily relate to using a cellular phone while driving.

### (B)

(5) Please use the following safety guidelines while driving with a cellular phone. (6) Making driving your top priority. (7) If a phone call will distract you, pull over to the side of the road to handle it. (8) Or, if you have a passenger in the car, hand the phone briefly to he or she. (9) Use speed dial or redial on your phone to reduce the amount of time spent with fingers on the keypad, and position your phone within easy reach. (10) Suspend conversations during hazardous driving conditions. (11) Remember that any call you maked unsafely was a call that should have waited.

1. Sentence 1: **We are pleased that you have selected PortoPhone for you cellular phone needs.**

   What correction should be made to sentence 1?

   (1) change *are* to *is*
   (2) change *are* to *were*
   (3) change *have selected* to *will be selected*
   (4) change *you cellular* to *your cellular*
   (5) change *needs* to *need's*

2. Sentence 2: **For people on the go, a portable phone has become an essential tool for keeping in contact in both their personal and professional live's.**

   What correction should be made to sentence 2?

   (1) change *has* to *had*
   (2) change *become* to *became*
   (3) change *their* to *they're*
   (4) change *live's* to *lives*
   (5) no correction is necessary

3. Sentence 3: **While we believe in the importance of this form of communication, there is also some potential dangers that we are obligated to discuss with you.**

   What correction should be made to sentence 3?

   (1) change *believe* to *believed*
   (2) change *believe* to *believes*
   (3) change *is* to *was*
   (4) change *is* to *are*
   (5) change *are* to *were*

4. Sentence 6: <u>**Making driving your**</u> **top priority.**

   Which is the best way to write the underlined portion of the text? If the original is the best way, choose option (1).

   (1) Making driving your
   (2) Having made driving your
   (3) Make driving your
   (4) Making driving you
   (5) Made driving your

5. Sentence 8: **Or, if you have a passenger in the car, hand the phone briefly to he or she.**

   What correction should be made to sentence 8?

   (1) change *you* to *your*
   (2) change *have* to *had*
   (3) change *hand* to *handing*
   (4) change *he* to *you*
   (5) change *he or she* to *him or her*

6. Sentence 11: **Remember that any call <u>you maked unsafely was</u> a call that should have waited.**

   Which of is the best way to write the underlined portion of the text? If the original is the best way, choose option (1).

   (1) you maked unsafely was
   (2) your maked unsafely was
   (3) you made unsafely was
   (4) you maked unsafely were
   (5) you maked unsafely been

*Questions 7–12 refer to the following letter.*

Dear Mrs. Fitzgerald:

**(A)**

(1) I regret to inform you that I will no longer be able to rent an apartment to you and your son as of January 1, 2003. (2) You and him have been wonderful renters in this building, and I will miss seeing you come and go. (3) However, I am almost 80 years old, and the time has arrive for me to sell my building. (4) I hope you understand that this process is difficult for me too.

**(B)**

(5) The building, along with the land and parking lot, have been sold to Marco Company, a large real estate development enterprise. (6) It will be my understanding that this company plans to convert the apartments into four luxury condominiums. (7) Everyone who lives in the apartments now are required to vacate the premises by December 31.

**(C)**

(8) I know that this information is unpleasant, Mrs. Fitzgerald. (9) Neither you nor your son deserve news like this after being such steadfast residents here for so long. (10) Please be assured that I am doing everything possible to find you a suitable place to live as soon as possible.

Sincerely,

Walter Moss

7. Sentence 2: <u>You and him have been</u> wonderful renters in this building, and I will miss seeing you come and go.

Which is the best way to write the underlined portion of the text? If the original is the best way, choose option (1).

(1) You and him have been
(2) You and he have been
(3) You and him has been
(4) You and him will have been
(5) You and they have been

8. Sentence 3: However, I am almost 80 years old, and the time has arrive for me to sell my building.

What correction should be made to sentence 3?

(1) change *am* to *is*
(2) change *has* to *have*
(3) change *arrive* to *arriving*
(4) change *arrive* to *arrived*
(5) change *me* to *I*

9. Sentence 5: The building, along with the land and parking lot, <u>have been sold</u> to Marco Company, a large real estate development enterprise.

Which is the best way to write the underlined portion of the text? If the original is the best way, choose option (1).

(1) have been sold
(2) has been sold
(3) been sold
(4) had been sold
(5) will have been sold

10. Sentence 6: It will be my understanding that this company plans to convert the apartments into four luxury condominiums.

What correction should be made to sentence 6?

(1) change *will be* to *is*
(2) change *will be* to *be*
(3) change *plans* to *plan*
(4) change *plans* to *plan's*
(5) no correction is necessary

11. Sentence 7: Everyone who lives in the apartments now are required to vacate the premises by December 31.

What correction should be made to sentence 7?

(1) change *lives* to *living*
(2) change *are* to *is*
(3) change *are* to *were*
(4) change *required* to *require*
(5) no correction is necessary

12. Sentence 9: Neither you nor <u>your son deserve news</u> like this after being such steadfast residents here for so long.

Which is the best way to write the underlined portion of the text? If the original is the best way, choose option (1).

(1) your son deserve news
(2) you son deserve news
(3) you're son deserve news
(4) your son deserves news
(5) your son deserve new's

*Answers are on page 128.*

# Combining Sentences

*Language Arts, Writing pages 83–114*
*Complete GED pages 105–134*

## Compound Sentences

A correctly written **compound sentence** joins two independent clauses, uses a coordinating conjunction that makes sense, and has a comma before the conjunction.

<u>Get to work on time</u>, **or** <u>you will lose your job</u>.

<small>INDEPENDENT CLAUSE</small>          <small>INDEPENDENT CLAUSE</small>

### EXERCISE 1

<u>Part A</u>      **Directions:**   Read each pair of sentences below. Circle the conjunction that makes the most sense in joining the sentences. Then, on the line provided, combine the sentences using a comma correctly.

1. *(and, but)*
   It was a beautiful day outside. The man carried his umbrella anyway.

   _____

2. *(so, or)*
   The store has closed for the day. All employees can punch out and go.

   _____

3. *(so, yet)*
   She is studying for the real estate license exam. She can become a real estate agent.

   _____

4. *(but, for)*
   We would love to hire a candidate like this one. He would fit in well here.

   _____

5. *(or, so)*
   You can pick up an application at the bank. You can have an application mailed to you.

   _____

6. *(and, or)*
   I am qualified for the job posted. I would like to apply for it.

   _____

**Part B**    **Directions:**    Some of the compound sentences below are correct as written. Some have errors. If the sentence is correct, write a *C* in the blank provided. If the sentence is incorrect, write the number of the following requirement that is missing. Then correct the sentence.

A correctly written compound sentence

(1) joins two independent clauses.
(2) uses a coordinating conjunction that makes sense.
(3) has a comma before the conjunction.

1. The administrative assistant answers phones, and does all typing.

_____

2. Winter is my favorite season, for I love to ski and ice skate.

_____

3. Your order has been received and it will be shipped on Wednesday.

_____

4. She was writing a letter home, but forgot to mail it.

_____

5. The floors are covered with dog hair and shoe marks, but they look dirty.

_____

6. The assembly line has slowed down, and the shift supervisor looks angry.

_____

7. The bonus in his paycheck was a surprise and he appreciated it greatly.

_____

8. The printer is out of paper, or I will add more.

_____

9. The landscaper surveyed the yard, and recommended weed control.

_____

10. The book has just been published and the author is on a sales tour.

_____

*Answers are on page 128.*

# Run-on Sentences and Comma Splices

A **run-on sentence** occurs when two complete clauses are joined without a conjunction.

| | |
|---|---|
| **Run-on:** | The flight has been delayed we won't go to the airport yet. |
| **Correct:** | The flight has been delayed, **so** we won't go to the airport yet. |

A **comma splice** incorrectly joins two sentences with just a comma.

| | |
|---|---|
| **Comma splice:** | He called the police, they came right away. |
| **Correct:** | He called the police, **and** they came right away. |

### EXERCISE 2

**Directions:** Correct the run-on sentences and comma splices below. If the sentence is correct as written, write a *C* in the blank provided.

1. Our weekend dishwasher did not show up for work the night manager has to fill in. _____

2. Please let us know what size hotel room you will be needing, decide what your arrival and departure dates will be. _____

3. The sales report indicates another successful quarter this is good news considering how much we have invested. _____

4. I enjoyed the presentation the film was also excellent and informative. _____

5. He looked terrific in that new suit at your mother's wedding. _____

6. The package was shipped via overnight mail, it should arrive before noon tomorrow. _____

7. Juanita schedules all employee vacations her assistant Fred distributes the information. _____

8. Every book on this shelf needs to be relabeled and reorganized. _____

9. Tanya wrote the pages, Samuel edited them. _____

10. Football is his favorite spectator sport he hates to actually play it. _____

*Answers are on page 128.*

# Complex Sentences

A **complex sentence** contains a dependent clause joined to an independent clause. If the dependent clause comes first in the sentence, a comma should follow it.

<u>Because you woke up earlier,</u> <u>you should make the coffee.</u>
          DEPENDENT CLAUSE                 INDEPENDENT CLAUSE

<u>You should make the coffee</u> <u>because you woke up earlier.</u>
          INDEPENDENT CLAUSE           DEPENDENT CLAUSE

## EXERCISE 3

<u>Part A</u>    **Directions:**    Combine each pair of clauses with a subordinating conjunction from the list below. If the dependent clause comes first in the sentence, be sure to follow it with a comma.

| | | | |
|---|---|---|---|
| before | because | if | where |
| after | since | unless | wherever |
| while | so that | whether | though |
| when | in order that | | although |
| as soon as | | | even though |
| as long as | | | |
| until | | | |

1. the phone rang

   no one answered it

   _____

2. you will eat dinner with us each night

   you are living in our house

   _____

3. you are allowed to have up to three telephones

   you have signed up for Family Plan Plus

   _____

4. Bessie signed the enclosed documents

   she did not agree with the terms stated

   _____

5. my assistant will make the necessary corrections

   there are mistakes

   _____

6. Manuel was looking for a job

   his wife could not leave the house

   _____

7. he asked for the check

   we finished our meal

   _____

8. the new offices look really sharp

   the renovation was not expensive

   _____

9. Sue asked for raises for her entire department

   we saw an extra $20–$30 in our paychecks last month

   _____

10. my father arrives at home

    he is surrounded by four screaming children

    _____

<u>Part B</u>      **Directions:**   Correct the complex sentence errors in the passage below. Some sentences may be correct as written.

When you change your place of employment you may be in the position of wondering what to do with the money you have accumulated in your retirement account. One option is to "roll over" the money into a new retirement account, so that you will not have to pay taxes on that money. Or since you prefer, you can withdraw the money in one lump sum and pay taxes on it. Taking the lump sum also might require you to pay a "premature withdrawal" penalty of up to 10 percent.

It is always a good idea to consult with a tax advisor, before you make any financial decisions of this magnitude. You have worked hard to earn this money so you should take good care of it.

*Answers are on page 129.*

# Dependent Clauses in a Paragraph

Some sentence fragments can be difficult to detect because they are part of a paragraph that makes sense. Remember to look at each sentence independently and be sure it has a subject and verb and expresses a complete thought.

**EXERCISE 4**

**Directions:** Underline the subordinating conjunctions in each paragraph below. Correct any sentence fragments by connecting dependent clauses to nearby sentences.

1. Please be sure to punch in. When you arrive at the job site. We are finding that some employees are not punching in until after their first break. This creates a problem for the administration. Because there is a discrepancy between actual time worked and recorded time.

2. Will you please send me a copy of my apartment lease? When I signed it, I forgot to keep a copy for myself. I understand that I will need it. When I apply for residency rates at school this fall. Your immediate attention is requested, and I thank you for your assistance.

3. The stories you have sent us for possible publication in our magazine are very effective. However, we do not have a need for fiction at this time. Please consider sending us some general-interest nonfiction pieces. If you would like. Our magazine is always interested in finding talented new writers.

4. Your payment is due, Ms. Morgan. As soon as the bill is received. We will be forced to shut off your cable service if we do not receive a check for $82.50 by Monday. Although we value you as a customer. We cannot delay action any longer.

5. Travel now and receive over $200 in extra benefits. We will send you dinner certificates, discount coupons for museums, and two-for-one offers from many leading merchants in town. Unless you call now. You will miss out on this great offer from TravelPro.com.

*Answers are on page 129.*

# GED Sentence Construction

Some items on Part I of the GED Language Arts, Writing Test will require you to change the pattern of a sentence or combine two sentences. The new sentence should have the same meaning as the original.

**EXERCISE 5**

**Directions:** Choose the best answer to each question below.

1. **The factory floor has just been cleaned and waxed. Be careful when you walk across it.**

   The most effective combination of these sentences would include which group of words?

   (1) cleaned and waxed unless be careful when you walk
   (2) cleaned, waxed, and be careful when you walk
   (3) cleaned and waxed, so be careful when you walk
   (4) cleaned and waxed, although be careful when you walk
   (5) cleaned and waxed, but be careful when you walk

2. **The computers on the third floor are all down, but those on eight can be used if your staff needs them.**

   If you rewrote the sentence beginning with

   *Although the computers on the third floor are all down,*

   the next word should be

   (1) so
   (2) but
   (3) if
   (4) those
   (5) use

3. **When she had been driving for more than four hours, she decided to take a quick break.**

   If you rewrote the sentence beginning with

   *She had been driving for more than four hours,*

   the next word should be

   (1) but
   (2) and
   (3) although
   (4) if
   (5) she

4. **You could invest in the stock market. You could put the money in a savings account.**

   The most effective combination of these sentences would include which group of words?

   (1) stock market, so you
   (2) stock market even though
   (3) stock market, if you
   (4) stock market unless you
   (5) stock market, or you

5. **Sales for this product have skyrocketed because new ads were run on TV and radio.**

   If you rewrote the sentence beginning with

   *Since new ads were run on television and the radio,*

   the next word(s) should be

   (1) because
   (2) even though
   (3) sales
   (4) skyrocketed
   (5) for

*Answers are on page 129.*

# Sequence of Tenses

The logical relationship between verbs in a sentence is called **sequence of tenses.**

## EXERCISE 6

**Directions:** Choose the best answer to each question below.

1. **They <u>talk</u> when you asked for quiet.**

   Which is the best way to write the underlined portion of the text? If the original is the best way, choose option (1).

   (1) talk
   (2) will talk
   (3) had talked
   (4) were talking
   (5) are talking

2. **After the foreman <u>blows</u> the whistle, the workers will shut down the machines.**

   Which is the best way to write the underlined portion of the text? If the original is the best way, choose option (1).

   (1) blows
   (2) was blowing
   (3) had blown
   (4) blew
   (5) did blow

3. **If the customer had asked for service, I <u>will respond</u> immediately.**

   Which is the best way to write the underlined portion of the text? If the original is the best way, choose option (1).

   (1) will respond
   (2) respond
   (3) responded
   (4) will have responded
   (5) would have responded

4. **When the weather is favorable, most of the fishermen <u>were working</u> six or seven days per week.**

   Which is the best way to write the underlined portion of the text? If the original is the best way, choose option (1).

   (1) were working
   (2) work
   (3) had worked
   (4) worked
   (5) will have worked

*Answers are on page 130.*

# Combining Sentences

**Directions:** Choose the <u>one best answer</u> to each question. Some of the sentences may contain errors. A few sentences, however, may be correct as written. Read the sentences carefully and then answer the questions based on them. For each question, choose the answer that would result in the most effective writing of the sentence or sentences.

*Questions 1–7 refer to the following notice.*

### Sign Up Now for the Walk for Heart Health

**(A)**

(1) Thousands of people have already registered for the fourth annual Walk for Heart Health fundraiser. (2) It's not too late for you. (3) The walk is scheduled for July 18, but the deadline for signing up to participate is June 30. (4) Three easy ways to register are described below.

**(B)**

(5) One way is to register online by visiting www.Heartwalk.org. (6) Although you have a credit card, this method is probably the easiest. (7) Just follow the convenient instructions on your computer screen you are ready to walk! (8) Another easy registration method is by telephone. (9) Call 1-800-555-1212, and a HeartWalk volunteer will take down the necessary information. (10) Finally, you can pick up a registration form downtown. (11) When you stop by Midmarket stores or Plus Pizza Parlors.

**(C)**

(12) The annual Walk for Heart Health is a terrific way to support numerous programs that focus on the prevention of heart disease. (13) By participating in the walk, you had helped thousands of people who are in need. (14) In addition, you'll strengthen your own heart by walking the 20-mile route!

1. **Sentences 1 and 2: Thousands of people have already registered for the fourth annual Walk for Heart Health fundraiser. It's not too late for you.**

   The most effective combination of sentences 1 and 2 would include which group of words?

   (1) fundraiser because it's not
   (2) fundraiser it's not
   (3) fundraiser, it's not
   (4) fundraiser if it's not
   (5) fundraiser, but it's not

2. **Sentence 3: The walk is scheduled for July 18, but the deadline for signing up to participate is June 30.**

   If you rewrote sentence 3 beginning with

   *The deadline for signing up to participate is June 30*

   the next words should be

   (1) so that the walk is
   (2) although the walk is
   (3) the walk is
   (4) the walk was
   (5) if the walk is

3. **Sentence 6: <u>Although you have a credit card,</u> this method is probably the easiest.**

   Which is the best way to write the underlined portion of the text? If the original is the best way, choose option (1).

   (1) Although you have a credit card, this
   (2) Although you have a credit card this
   (3) If you have a credit card, this
   (4) So that you have a credit card, this
   (5) You have a credit card, this

4. **Sentence 7: Just follow the convenient instructions on your computer <u>screen you are</u> ready to walk!**

   Which is the best way to write the underlined portion of the text? If the original is the best way, choose option (1).

   (1) screen you are
   (2) screen, you are
   (3) screen even though you are
   (4) screen because you are
   (5) screen, and you are

5. **Sentence 9: Call 1-800-555-1212, and a HeartWalk volunteer will take down the necessary information.**

   What correction should be made to sentence 9?

   (1) remove the comma before *and*
   (2) change *and* to *but*
   (3) change *and* to *if*
   (4) change *and* to *though*
   (5) no correction is necessary

6. **Sentences 10 and 11: Finally, you can pick up a registration form <u>downtown. When you stop</u> by Midmarket stores or Plus Pizza Parlors.**

   Which is the best way to write the underlined portion of the text? If the original is the best way, choose option (1).

   (1) downtown.  When you stop
   (2) downtown when you stop
   (3) downtown, when you stop
   (4) downtown though you stop
   (5) downtown, but you stop

7. **Sentence 13: By participating in the walk, you had helped thousands of people who are in need.**

   What correction should be made to sentence 13?

   (1) change *participating* to *participate*
   (2) remove the comma after *walk*
   (3) change *had helped* to *were helping*
   (4) change *had helped* to *will help*
   (5) no correction is necessary

   *Answers are on page 130.*

# Cumulative Review

**Directions:** Choose the <u>one best answer</u> to each question. Some of the sentences may contain errors in organization, sentence structure, usage, and mechanics. A few sentences, however, may be correct as written. Read the sentences carefully and then answer the questions based on them. For each question, choose the answer that would result in the most effective writing of the sentence or sentences.

*Questions 1–7 refer to the following bulletin.*

## Downtown Community Partnership for Children

**(A)**

(1) The Downtown Community Partnership for Children is an organization created in 1984 to ensure that all families has access to quality early childhood programs. (2) It is our intention to make certain that all children living in the greater Hartford area begin kindergarten ready to learn. (3) When community leaders, local businesses, early childhood professionals, and parents pool their resources good things happen for children.

**(B)**

(4) There is many benefits for parents who take advantage of this community partnership. (5) Tuition subsidies are offered to those family's who fall within certain income guidelines. (6) Education specialists have established an extensive lending library of books, videos, and pamphlets that are available free of charge to all partnership parents. (7) In addition, free workshops dealing with issues such as discipline, violence in the media, and family health are held frequently. (8) Finally, all children in a partnership program receives a free annual physical prior to entering one of our programs.

**(C)**

(9) Parents and families are not the only ones who benefit from the Downtown Community Partnership for Children. (10) Early childhood educator's receive benefits such as tuition reimbursement for college courses in the field, monetary grants to purchase materials for their classrooms, and extra time off to attend partnership-sponsored lectures and workshops. (11) Businesses that support the partnership may receive certain tax benefits they get free advertising in program brochures. (12) An organization like the Downtown Community Partnership for Children truly benefits everyone in the community.

1. Sentence 1: **The Downtown Community Partnership for Children is an organization created in 1984 to ensure that all families has access to quality early childhood programs.**

   What correction should be made to sentence 1?

   (1) insert a comma after *Children*
   (2) insert a comma after *ensure*
   (3) replace *families* with *family's*
   (4) change *has* to *had*
   (5) change *has* to *have*

2. Sentence 3: **When community leaders, local businesses, early childhood professionals, and parents pool their resources good things happen for children.**

   What correction should be made to sentence 3?

   (1) change *parents* to *parent's*
   (2) insert a comma after *resources*
   (3) change *happen* to *happens*
   (4) change *happen* to *happened*
   (5) no correction is necessary

3. Sentence 4: <u>**There is many benefits for parents who take**</u> **advantage of this community partnership.**

   Which is the best way to write the underlined portion of the text? If the original is the best way, choose option (1).

   (1) There is many benefits for parents who take
   (2) There was many benefits for parents who take
   (3) There is many benefits for parents who took
   (4) There was many benefits for parents who took
   (5) There are many benefits for parents who take

4. Sentence 5: **Tuition subsidies are offered to those family's who fall within certain income guidelines.**

   What correction should be made to sentence 5?

   (1) change *are* to *is*
   (2) change *offered* to *offering*
   (3) change *family's* to *families*
   (4) change *fall* to *falls*
   (5) no correction is necessary

5. Sentence 8: **Finally, all children in a partnership program receives a free annual physical prior to entering one of our programs.**

   What correction should be made to sentence 8?

   (1) change *receives* to *receive*
   (2) change *receives* to *received*
   (3) change *entering* to *have entered*
   (4) change *our* to *us*
   (5) no correction is necessary

6. Sentence 10: **Early childhood <u>educator's receive benefits</u> such as tuition reimbursement for college courses in the field, monetary grants to purchase materials for their classrooms, and extra time off to attend partnership-sponsored lectures and workshops.**

   Which is the best way to write the underlined portion of the text? If the original is the best way, choose option (1).

   (1) educator's receive benefits
   (2) educators receive benefits
   (3) educator's received benefits
   (4) educator's will receive benefits
   (5) educator's had received benefits

7. Sentence 11: **Businesses that support the partnership <u>may receive certain tax benefits they get</u> free advertising in program brochures.**

   Which is the best way to write the underlined portion of the text? If the original is the best way, choose option (1).

   (1) may receive certain tax benefits they get
   (2) may receive certain tax benefits they got
   (3) may have received certain tax benefits they get
   (4) may receive certain tax benefits, if they get
   (5) may receive certain tax benefits, and they get

*Questions 8–13 refer to the following letter.*

June 30, 2002

Dear Mr. and Mrs. Wentworth:

**(A)**

(1) It will be nice to meet with you last Thursday to discuss the renovation plans you have in mind for your home.  (2) I hope I have convinced you that Peters & Sons Plumbing is the right company for the job.  (3) We have over fifteen years of experience in the home improvement industry.  (4) We been doing handicapped-accessible bathrooms since the early 1990s.

**(B)**

(5) As I promised, enclosed are a detailed estimate of costs for the job.  (6) The total cost of $2,480 includes all labor and materials. (7) We recommend that you go to House Plus to choose your fixtures and tile.  (8) Because this store has a great selection at a very good value.  (9) Everyone think House Plus is the place to go.

**(C)**

(10) Either my son or I plan to be on the job site every day so that you can be assured of excellent supervision of the crew.  (11) We know you will be pleased with the quality of our work.  (12) I have included a list of people for whom we have done work, but any one of them will be happy to talk with you about our qualifications.

Sincerely,

James Peters

8. **Sentence 1: It will be nice to meet with you last Thursday to discuss the renovation plans you have in mind for your home.**

   What correction should be made to sentence 1?

   (1) replace *It* with *They*
   (2) change *will be* to *was*
   (3) change *will be* to *is*
   (4) change *have* to *has*
   (5) change *have* to *had*

9. **Sentence 4: <u>We been doing</u> handicapped-accessible bathrooms since the early 1990s.**

   Which is the best way to write the underlined portion of the text?  If the original is the best way, choose option (1).

   (1) We been doing
   (2) They been doing
   (3) We have been doing
   (4) We had been doing
   (5) We will be doing

10. **Sentence 5: As I promised, enclosed are a detailed estimate of costs for the job.**

What correction should be made to sentence 5?

(1) change *promised* to *promise*
(2) remove the comma after *promised*
(3) change *are* to *were*
(4) change *are* to *is*
(5) no correction is necessary

11. **Sentences 7 and 8: We recommend that you go to House Plus to choose your fixtures and tile. Because this store has a great selection at a very good value.**

The most effective combination of sentences 7 and 8 would include which group of words?

(1) your fixtures and tile. Since this store has
(2) your fixtures and tile, because this store has
(3) your fixtures and tile, but this store has
(4) your fixtures and tile because this store has
(5) your fixtures and tile although this store has

12. **Sentence 9: Everyone think House Plus is the place to go.**

What correction should be made to sentence 9?

(1) change *think* to *thinks*
(2) change *think* to *thought*
(3) change *think* to *will think*
(4) change *is* to *are*
(5) change *is* to *was*

13. **Sentence 12: I have included a list of people for whom <u>we have done work, but</u> any one of them will be happy to talk with you about our qualifications.**

Which is the best way to write the underlined portion of the text? If the original is the best way, choose option (1).

(1) we have done work, but
(2) we have done work although
(3) we have done work, and
(4) we had done work, but
(5) we will have done work, but

*Answers are on page 130.*

 Go to **www.GEDWriting.com** for additional practice and instruction!

# Organization

Language Arts, Writing pages 115–143
Complete GED pages 153–168

## Effective Paragraphs

A **paragraph** is a group of sentences that communicates one idea. A **topic sentence** states the main idea. The other sentences add supporting details to this main idea.

### EXERCISE 1

**Directions:** Read each group of sentences below and decide if it is a paragraph. Write *yes* or *no* in the space provided.

_____ 1.    Here are the details about your upcoming stay at East Bay Motel. Check-in time is any time after 3:00 P.M., and check-out time is before 11:00 A.M. Your credit card will be billed at the time of your reservation. If you find it necessary to cancel your reservation, you must do so three days prior to scheduled arrival, or you will be billed for the full cost of the room.

_____ 2.    As the demand for overnight package deliveries grows, so does the demand for driving personnel. If you are age 21 or older, and you have a valid driver's license, you might consider checking out this growing field of employment. The pay is excellent, and many delivery companies are now offering flexible working hours and other benefits.

_____ 3.    This letter is sent to inform you that you are eligible for a $1,000 cash bonus if you act now. Money is tight these days. The cost of your clock repair is $26.90. When my father was young, he delivered newspapers to more than 300 homes each morning.

_____ 4.    In many areas of rural America, firefighters do not get paid. Many of them also purchase their own equipment, such as beepers, flashing lights, and protective clothing. These volunteer firefighters may spend as much as 20 hours per week answering calls, maintaining trucks, and attending training sessions. Furthermore, they risk injury or even death because they care so deeply about their communities.

_____ 5.    There is a growing push in education today to require all students to use a laptop computer during the school day and at home as well. Homework can be a daunting task for many children, especially those without an adult at home to help out. Summer camp is a wonderful opportunity for kids to learn new skills in a relaxed, slow-paced environment. Without two incomes, many families would barely scrape by economically.

*Answers are on page 130.*

# Inserting a Topic Sentence

Some questions on the GED Language Arts, Writing Test will require you to choose an effective topic sentence for a paragraph. Remember that the topic sentence should summarize the main idea of all the sentences in the paragraph.

**EXERCISE 2**

**Directions:** Choose the one best answer to each question.

1.     For example, a roommate, like a brother or a sister, is likely to borrow your clothes without asking. And what happens if it turns out that your roommate does not care to clean up after himself or herself? In addition, figuring out who pays what bills and when can be a major source of disagreement. There are bound to be many difficult issues that will arise no matter how compatible two people are.

   Which sentence below would be most effective at the beginning of this paragraph?

   (1) Though having a roommate can save you money, this kind of living situation is not completely problem free.
   (2) Roommates are more like siblings than like a spouse or parent.
   (3) Sharing clothes is one advantage to having a roommate, despite the hassles that accompany this arrangement.
   (4) There are all kinds of problems in every kind of living situation.
   (5) Finding a suitable roommate is hard work but worth the effort.

2.     Your payment is overdue for the fourth time this year. You have failed to make alternative payment plans even though our accounting representative has tried to contact you several times. You have not returned our phone calls. We can no longer afford to keep you on as a valued credit-card customer.

   Which sentence below would be most effective at the beginning of this paragraph?

   (1) We at First Bank invite you to become a premier cardholder by filling out the enclosed application.
   (2) Customers are often late with their credit-card payments.
   (3) Credit cards are a convenient, safe, and relatively inexpensive way to pay most of your bills.
   (4) We regret to inform you that First Bank has canceled your credit card.
   (5) Customers at First Bank receive top-quality service and many other benefits.

3.  First, log on to the Web site listed in the manual. Click on the Easy Reference Guide and follow the prompts given. Once you have found the model number of the camera you are using, you can follow the easy troubleshooting directions to solve most operational problems. If, after consulting the online reference guide, you are still having trouble with the camera, call customer service at 1-800-555-3869.

Which sentence below would be most effective at the beginning of this paragraph?

(1) The Internet is an efficient and easy path to lots of useful information.
(2) Cameras, like most electronic equipment, are difficult to repair and maintain unless you have some basic skills.
(3) Here are the steps to take if you are having trouble with the operation of your new camera.
(4) We recently purchased a new camera from your Web site, and we are interested in getting some information about its use.
(5) Use the Internet to solve many simple problems—with no need for repair or maintenance manuals.

4.  Because of vaccinations, there are substantially fewer cases of these diseases today than several decades ago. Tetanus is a serious disease caused by a germ that enters the body through a cut or wound. Diphtheria, spread from an infected person to the nose or throat of another, can lead to breathing problems, heart failure, paralysis, and even death. There would be many more cases of these diseases if we stopped vaccinating people.

Which sentence below would be most effective at the beginning of this paragraph?

(1) Today there are vaccines that can prevent diseases such as mumps, chicken pox, measles, and rubella.
(2) Vaccination is the best way to protect against tetanus and diphtheria.
(3) There are some risks to vaccinations that patients should be aware of.
(4) It is a good idea to find out which vaccinations are covered under your company's health plan.
(5) Tetanus causes serious, painful spasms of the muscles in the body.

5.  All merchandise will be at least 25 percent off, including items previously marked down. Shop now for those hot summer events on your calendar! Choose from hundreds of shirts, shorts, dresses, and shoes—all of excellent quality at exceptional savings. The sale begins Friday morning at 8:00 and continues until 6:00 P.M. Sunday at Fancy's Fashions.

Which sentence below would be most effective at the beginning of this paragraph?

(1) Saving money on clothing is possible if you budget and shop wisely.
(2) All major appliances are on sale now at Eastham Electric.
(3) All store employees should prepare their departments for the end-of-summer sale.
(4) When you shop at Fancy's Fashions, you will find everything you need.
(5) You are invited to save lots of money on quality clothing at Fancy's Fashions.

*Answers are on page 130.*

# Dividing and Rearranging Paragraphs

Sometimes a paragraph may need to be divided into two paragraphs. Other times, the sentences within a piece of writing may need to be rearranged to make more sense.

## EXERCISE 3

**Directions:** Choose the one best answer to each question.

1.
                                    **(A)**

   (1) Many products containing seaweed are used by people every day. (2) Seaweed extracts are used in toothpaste, shaving cream, ice cream, and salad dressing, among many other things. (3) People are often surprised to learn just how prevalent seaweed is as an additive in foods and skin-care products. (4) Although there is a big market for seaweed, companies in the United States have not been producing it. (5) However, recent discoveries may make seaweed farming profitable along certain stretches of the North Carolina coast. (6) A process called cell culturing speeds up the reproduction of seaweed. (7) Scientists at several U.S. companies are learning how to use this process to grow profits.

Which revision would make paragraph A more effective?

Begin a new paragraph

(1)  with sentence 2
(2)  with sentence 3
(3)  with sentence 4
(4)  with sentence 5
(5)  with sentence 6

2.
                                    **(A)**

   (1) What are some good ways for parents to help children eat healthfully and avoid obesity? (2) Here are some suggestions that physicians and nutritionists recommend. (3) First, don't use food as a bribe or reward for good behavior. (4) Don't push youngsters into trying new foods, "cleaning" their plates, or eating foods in a particular order.

                                    **(B)**

   (5) Finally, don't introduce the concept of "dieting" to any child. (6) The best way to help children develop a healthful relationship with food is to develop one for yourself. (7) Have lots of nutritious foods in your home and let your child see you enjoying them in moderation. (8) Avoid making disparaging remarks about your eating patterns or your body shape. (9) Get lots of exercise and have lots of conversations about what makes for a long, healthy life.

Which revision would improve this piece of writing?

(1)  combine paragraphs A and B
(2)  move sentence 9 to follow sentence 1
(3)  move sentence 5 to the end of paragraph A
(4)  move sentence 7 to the end of paragraph A
(5)  no revision is necessary

*Answers are on page 130.*

# Deleting Unnecessary Sentences

Some questions on the GED Language Arts, Writing Test will give you the option of removing a sentence from a paragraph to make the writing more effective.

**EXERCISE 4**

**Directions:** Choose the one best answer to each question.

*Questions 1–4 refer to the following letter.*

Dear Mr. Reynolds:

**(A)**

(1) Thank you for sending us your résumé. (2) We at PharmCo are always looking for bright young college graduates to help us become an even better company. (3) As you know, we are a leader in the health-care support field, and we aim to become number one in the world by the year 2010. (4) We are happy to hear of your interest in joining us on this quest.

**(B)**

(5) From your résumé, it appears that you are most interested in a position in our technology department. (6) Your experiences as a lab technician and computer analyst would be extremely valuable in the innovative work we are doing in our labs right now. (7) One of our current lab assistants graduated three years ago from Georgia Tech. (8) Fortunately, we now have several openings for which you would be qualified.

**(C)**

(9) We would like to invite you to begin our interviewing and hiring process. (10) You may call our Human Resources Manager at ext. 223 and set up an appointment to spend a morning with us. (11) During this morning, you will tour our facility, meet with several executives, and fill out an application. (12) Interviewing for a new job can be a very stressful process. (13) If all goes well during this morning visit, we will call you to set up a final day of interviews the following week.

**(D)**

(14) Thank you again for your interest in PharmCo, Mr. Reynolds. (15) I must tell you that we receive hundreds of résumés every week, and we extend an interview invitation to only a small fraction of these. (16) You should be proud of your accomplishments. (17) PharmCo is a publicly traded company on the New York Stock Exchange. (18) We look forward to hearing from you and exploring your possible future employment at PharmCo.

Regards,

Joan Sanchez,

Technology Lab Manager

1. Which revision would make paragraph A more effective?

   (1) remove sentence 1
   (2) remove sentence 3
   (3) remove sentence 3
   (4) remove sentence 4
   (5) no revision is necessary

2. Which revision would make paragraph B more effective?

   (1) remove sentence 5
   (2) remove sentence 6
   (3) remove sentence 7
   (4) remove sentence 8
   (5) no revision is necessary

3. Which revision would make paragraph C more effective?

   (1) remove sentence 9
   (2) remove sentence 10
   (3) remove sentence 11
   (4) remove sentence 12
   (5) remove sentence 13

4. Which revision would make paragraph D more effective?

   (1) remove sentence 14
   (2) remove sentence 15
   (3) remove sentence 16
   (4) remove sentence 17
   (5) remove sentence 18

*Answers are on page 130.*

# Tone and Diction

Some writing is casual in its tone and word choice. Other writing is more formal. Some questions on the GED Language Arts, Writing Test will require you to recognize and delete sentences that do not match the **tone** and **diction** of the rest of the paragraph.

**EXERCISE 5**

**Directions:** Underline the sentence that does not match the tone and diction of each paragraph below. If the paragraph is effective as written, write *effective* in the space provided.

1.      The easiest way to get from the wedding to the reception is to take a left turn out of the church parking lot and get on Route 28. Go about three miles and look for a sign on your right that says "Old Mill Reservoir." Commence to steer your motor vehicle in a southwesterly direction upon entrance to the aforesaid reservoir, keeping both hands firmly on the steering wheel of the vehicle. Once you're in the park, you'll see lots of signs for the Davis/Crespi wedding party!

_____

2.      The main reason for this note to is to inform you of a concern many of the neighbors share regarding how fast you drive down our street. We consider this a quiet, family-oriented neighborhood, and we value the safety of our children. On many occasions we have witnessed you traveling at unsafe speeds down the street and into your driveway. Although several of us have spoken to you about this problem, there has been no improvement in your driving. We are making this last-ditch effort to get you to clean up your act before we call the cops and have you dragged into court. Thank you so much for your attention to this important matter.

_____

3.      Every child under the age of 19 in this state can get free or low-cost health care. If your child or a child you know has not seen a doctor in the past year due to financial concerns, please call 1-888-555-0038 and speak to one of our health advocates. We will direct you to a clinic where the child can receive a confidential, thorough health screening.

_____

4.      Please accept my apology for my son Nathan's absence from his classes last week. We are having some family problems that prevented us from getting Nathan to school. His crabby old ma is sick as a dog and needs round-the-clock care, and Nathan is the man for the job. He will certainly be in school next week, as we have found a nurse for his mother.

_____

*Answers are on page 131.*

# Organization

**Directions:** Choose the <u>one best answer</u> to each question. Some of the sentences may contain errors. A few sentences, however, may be correct as written. Read the sentences carefully and then answer the questions based on them. For each question, choose the answer that would result in the most effective writing of the sentence or sentences.

*Questions 1–4 refer to the following business article.*

## Franchisee Profile: Jake Gupta

**(A)**

(1) As most people in this business know, a successful Best Burger franchise is based on one thing, and one thing only—the franchise owner. (2) True, the quality of the location is important, and financial resources are necessary as well, but these are minor factors compared to the quality of the owner in charge of the operation. (3) A good location is one in which there is high traffic with relatively low costs. (4) A good owner can turn a mediocre location into a gold mine, and Jake Gupta has done just that—with four Best Burger franchises.

**(B)**

(5) We recently visited Gupta in one of his shops, and we asked him what factors contributed to this award of a blue ribbon by the Regional Franchise Owners Association (RFOA) four years in a row. (6) "We focus on two things," said Gupta, "customer service and employee relations."

**(C)**

(7) The entire focus of a store's operation, he said, from product quality to cleanliness, is on pleasing the customer.

**(D)**

(8) Gupta and his business partners make sure that they share this commitment to service with all of their employees. (9) Every year they send their managers to RFOA training sessions that reinforce the importance of customer satisfaction. (10) They promote from within the organization, so their managers have been exposed to this service philosophy for many years. (11) In addition, they make sure that all employees are committed to meeting, and even exceeding, customer satisfaction goals.

**(E)**

(12) He offers bonuses to existing employees who refer applicants who succeed in the store. (13) He tries to make the work atmosphere fun and rewarding so that people enjoy coming in to work each day. (14) Finally, he has several trips and parties throughout the year that help to build employee morale.

1. Which revision would make paragraph A more effective?

   (1) move sentence 2 to the beginning of the paragraph
   (2) move sentence 3 to the beginning of the paragraph
   (3) remove sentence 3
   (4) remove sentence 4
   (5) no revision is necessary

2. **Sentence 7: The entire focus of a store's operation, he said, from product quality to cleanliness, is on pleasing the customer.**

   Which revision should be made to sentence 7?

   (1) move sentence 7 to follow sentence 1
   (2) move sentence 7 to follow sentence 2
   (3) move sentence 7 to the end of paragraph B
   (4) move sentence 7 to follow sentence 8
   (5) remove sentence 7

3. Which revision would make paragraph D more effective?

   (1) move sentence 8 to follow sentence 9
   (2) remove sentence 8
   (3) move sentence 9 to follow sentence 10
   (4) remove sentence 10
   (5) no revision is necessary

4. Which sentence below would be most effective at the beginning of paragraph E?

   (1) Gupta believes that location is just as important as customer service.
   (2) Gupta has found some creative ways to find and retain good staff.
   (3) Gupta finds that competition is tough in his area.
   (4) Gupta is a firm believer in paying new employees minimum wage.
   (5) Gupta has learned that customers can be difficult to please all the time.

   *Answers are on page 131.*

# Cumulative Review

**Directions:** Choose the <u>one best answer</u> to each question. Some of the sentences may contain errors in organization, sentence structure, usage, and mechanics. A few sentences, however, may be correct as written. Read the sentences carefully and then answer the questions based on them. For each question, choose the answer that would result in the most effective writing of the sentence or sentences.

*Questions 1–8 refer to the following travel brochure.*

### A Carefree Cruises Offer You More!

**(A)**

(1) Beginning July 1, you can experience the magic of a cruise vacation for less money than you would expect. (2) On board our newest ocean liner, the *Reditus Mare,* guests will enjoy luxury beyond belief at just a fraction of the cost of many comparable cruise vacations. (3) Imagining a visit to exciting Caribbean ports or a peaceful visit to a private beach hideaway. (4) If you are looking for the vacation of your dreams a Carefree Cruise is just right for you!

**(B)**

(5) On our popular Caribbean cruises, you explored the great mysteries of the sea. (6) Swimming and snorkeling alongside our trained guides, you'll see fish and plant life you have never seen before. (7) Professional botanists familiar with the area also offers several guided hikes through fascinating terrain at some of our remote ports of call. (8) Or paddle along the picturesque coast in one of our ocean kayaks—included in the cost of your cruise. (9) Looking for a more relaxed pace for your vacation? (10) We offer that too. (11) Enjoy the cooling sea breezes but you sit poolside on one our three decks. (12) Our chef can also prepare you a delicious picnic basket to take ashore for a private lunch. (13) You will find the personal attention of our hospitable staff to be efficient and courteous.

**(C)**

(14) Whether you spend a busy day full of activity or a quiet day of relaxation, you will no doubt enjoy a magnificent evening aboard the *Reditus Mare.* (15) Restaurants in the United States are generally excellent. (16) Dinner is served in two seatings, and the four-course meal prepared by our award-winning chefs will delight you. (17) After dinner, retire to your luxurious private cabin or choose to enjoy an evening of jazz in our comfortable lounge. (18) After you are rocked gently to sleep in your home away from home, you will awaken refreshed and ready for another fabulous day aboard the *Reditus Mare.*

1. **Sentence 3: <u>Imagining a visit</u> to exciting Caribbean ports or a peaceful visit to a private beach hideaway.**

   Which is the best way to write the underlined portion of the text? If the original is the best way, choose option (1).

   (1) Imagining a visit
   (2) Imagining, a visit
   (3) I was imagining a visit
   (4) He was imagining a visit
   (5) Imagine a visit

2. **Sentence 4: If you are looking for the vacation of your dreams a Carefree Cruise is just right for you!**

   What correction should be made to sentence 4?

   (1) change *you* to *your*
   (2) change *your* to *you're*
   (3) change *dreams* to *dream's*
   (4) insert a comma after *dreams*
   (5) insert a comma after *Cruise*

3. Sentence 5: **On our popular Caribbean cruises, you explored the great mysteries of the sea.**

   Which is the best way to write the underlined portion of the text? If the original is the best way, choose option (1).

   (1) cruises, you explored
   (2) cruises you explored
   (3) cruises, you will explore
   (4) cruises, you had explored
   (5) cruises, you are exploring

4. Sentence 7: **Professional botanists familiar with the area also offers several guided hikes through fascinating terrain at some of our remote ports of call.**

   What correction should be made to sentence 7?

   (1) change *offers* to *offer*
   (2) change *offers* to *offered*
   (3) change *our* to *ours*
   (4) change *our* to *my*
   (5) no correction is necessary

5. Which revision would make paragraph B more effective?

   Begin a new paragraph

   (1) with sentence 7
   (2) with sentence 8
   (3) with sentence 9
   (4) with sentence 10
   (5) with sentence 12

6. Sentence 11: **Enjoy the cooling <u>sea breezes but you sit</u> poolside on one our three decks.**

   Which is the best way to write the underlined portion of the text? If the original is the best way, choose option (1).

   (1) sea breeze but you sit
   (2) sea breeze, but you sit
   (3) sea breeze as you sit
   (4) sea breeze although you sit
   (5) sea breeze, because you sit

7. Sentence 15: **Restaurants in the United States are generally excellent.**

   Which revision should be made to sentence 15?

   (1) move sentence 15 to the end of paragraph A
   (2) move sentence 15 to the beginning of paragraph B
   (3) move sentence 15 to follow sentence 18
   (4) remove sentence 15
   (5) no revision is necessary

8. Sentence 18: **After you are rocked gently to sleep in your home away from home, you will awaken refreshed and ready for another fabulous day aboard the *Reditus Mare.***

   What correction should be made to sentence 18?

   (1) replace *After* with *Although*
   (2) remove the comma after *home*
   (3) change *you* to *he*
   (4) insert a comma after *ready*
   (5) no correction is necessary

*Questions 9–16 refer to the following memo.*

TO:     Postal Delivery Customers

FROM:  The Postmaster General

**(A)**

(1) From time to time, we find it necessary to remind our customers of our delivery procedures and restrictions. (2) Please take note of this information and keep it handy for future reference. (3) We are pleased to offer excellent service to you, our valued customers, and we hope that we are serving you're needs in the best way possible.

**(B)**

(4) Delivery times vary from neighborhood to neighborhood. (5) Although we try to be consistent from day to day, we <u>do not</u> guarantee regular delivery by any specific time. (6) If you usually receive your mail by a certain time, and it has not arrived by that time on a given day, forget about calling on the phone to rat on your delivery guy. (7) Our delivery schedule is affected by changes in personnel, weather, and route alterations. (8) Variations in your mail delivery time is something that should be expected.

**(C)**

(9) Please understand that postal workers are not required to deliver to a mailbox that is difficult to reach. (10) Common obstructions are things such as trash barrels, snow, or bicycles by keeping your mailbox and the path to it clear of these obstructions, you will be assured of regular mail delivery.

**(D)**

(11) The final reminder relates to priority and express deliveries as well as package delivery. (12) Priority mail will be delivered with your regular daily mail. (13) Express mail that is guaranteed delivery by noon arrived at your residence separately from your regular mail in most cases. (14) Occasionally, if express delivery coincides with a postal worker's route, you will receive all of your mail together. (15) Packages that fit on the regular mail truck is delivered with your regular mail. (16) Package delivery may take place separately from your regular mail if the package is oversized or during the holiday season.

9. Sentence 3: **We are pleased to offer excellent service to you, our valued customers, and we hope that we are serving you're needs in the best way possible.**

   What correction should be made to sentence 3?

   (1) change *are pleased* to *were pleased*
   (2) change *our* to *we*
   (3) change *hope* to *hoping*
   (4) change *you're* to *your*
   (5) no correction is necessary

10. Sentence 5: **Although we try to be consistent from day to day, we <u>do not</u> guarantee regular delivery by any specific time.**

    If you rewrote sentence 5 beginning with

    *We <u>do not</u> guarantee regular delivery by any specific time,*

    The next word should be

    (1) if
    (2) but
    (3) because
    (4) for
    (5) since

11. **Sentence 6: If you usually receive your mail by a certain time, and it has not arrived by that time on a given day, <u>forget about calling on the phone to rat on your delivery guy.</u>**

Which is the best way to write the underlined portion of the text? If the original is the best way, choose option (1).

(1) forget about calling on the phone to rat on your delivery guy.
(2) forgetting about calling on the phone to rat on your delivery guy
(3) to forget about calling on the phone to rat on your delivery guy.
(4) please do not rat on your delivery guy.
(5) please do not telephone us to report this.

12. **Sentence 8: Variations in your mail delivery time is something that should be expected.**

What correction should be made to sentence 8?

(1) change *Variations* to *Variation's*
(2) change *is* to *was*
(3) change *is* to *are*
(4) change *is* to *being*
(5) change *be* to *being*

13. Which sentence below would be most effective at the beginning of paragraph C?

(1) Mailboxes must be made of metal or durable wood that stands up to the weather.
(2) Trash pickup is usually earlier in the day than mail delivery.
(3) There are many requirements that must be fulfilled before a person can become a postal worker.
(4) Customers are a postal worker's number one priority.
(5) As a postal delivery customer, you are required to keep the area in front of your mailbox clear so that it is easily accessible by the postal worker.

14. **Sentence 10: Common obstructions are things such as trash barrels, snow, or <u>bicycles by keeping your mailbox and the path to it</u> clear of these obstructions, you will be assured of regular mail delivery.**

Which is the best way to write the underlined portion of the text? If the original is the best way, choose option (1).

(1) bicycles by keeping your mailbox and the path to it
(2) bicycles. By keeping your mailbox and the path to it
(3) bicycles to keep your mailbox and the path to it
(4) bicycles, by keeping your mailbox and the path to it
(5) bicycles. Keep your mailbox and the path to it

15. **Sentence 13: Express mail that is guaranteed delivery by noon arrived at your residence separately from your regular mail in most cases.**

What correction should be made to sentence 13?

(1) change *is* to *be*
(2) change *arrived* to *will arrive*
(3) change *arrived* to *will have arrived*
(4) insert a comma after *arrived*
(5) no correction is necessary

16. **Sentence 15: Packages that fit on the regular <u>mail truck is delivered with your</u> regular mail.**

Which is the best way to write the underlined portion of the text? If the original is the best way, choose option (1).

(1) mail truck is delivered with your
(2) mail truck is delivered with you're
(3) mail truck was delivered with your
(4) mail truck are delivered with your
(5) mail truck is being delivered with your

*Answers are on page 131.*

# Using Correct Language

*Language Arts, Writing pages 145–176*
*Complete GED pages 91–104; 126–134*

## Adjectives and Adverbs

An **adjective** is a word that describes a noun or pronoun. An **adverb** describes a verb, an adjective, or another adverb.

**EXERCISE 1**

**Directions:** Complete each sentence below by inserting an adverb or adjective in the blank.

1. _____, Mr. Petersen made the announcement over the loudspeaker.

2. The pet sitter arrived at the _____ apartment on time and ready to work.

3. Yesterday, the employees walked _____ into the office of their manager and demanded better working conditions.

4. We look forward to offering you _____ service throughout the holiday season.

5. We regretted the _____ performance at last night's concert.

6. When will you be able to bring your _____ baby here so we can meet her?

7. _____ the police officer turned the corner in pursuit of the suspect.

8. The elderly man slept _____ on the park bench by the river.

9. That computer looks too _____ and _____ to be of any use to us on this project.

10. The _____ teacher looked surprised when his students showed up unprepared for class.

*Answers are on page 131.*

# Misplaced Modifiers

A **modifying phrase** is a group of words that describes another word in a sentence. A modifying phrase answers questions such as *Who? What? When? Where? How? How much? What kind? How many?* or *Which one?* A modifying phrase should be placed as closely as possible to the word it describes.

**Incorrect:** Deleted unintentionally from the file, Ted had to retype the missing text.

**Correct:** Ted had to retype the missing text deleted unintentionally from the file.

**EXERCISE 2**

**Directions:** Rewrite each sentence below, correcting the misplaced modifier. Be sure to use commas when necessary. If the sentence has no error, write *correct* in the space provided.

1. Upset by all of the violence, tears streamed down the face of the old woman.

   _____

2. Cheering wildly, the calm president-elect began his speech to the convention crowd.

   _____

3. Sitting in the back of her closet, Margaret found the boxes she was looking for.

   _____

4. Wanting to be helpful, the man's supervisor gave him the rest of the day off.

   _____

5. Retail shops have been hiring hundreds of workers each day needing extra help for the holiday season.

   _____

6. The rude salesperson threw my sales receipt into the bag with a disgusted frown.

   _____

7. Falling gently to sleep, the soft music soothed the baby.

   _____

8. The computer disk fell to the floor with all my work saved on it.

   _____

*Answers are on page 132.*

# Dangling Modifiers

A **dangling modifier** is a word or phrase that has no word to describe in a sentence. To fix it, add a noun that makes sense and change the wording of the sentence slightly.

**Incorrect:** Irritated by the sound, earplugs were distributed.

**Correct:** Because we were irritated by the sound, earplugs were distributed.

**EXERCISE 3**

**Directions:** Rewrite each sentence below, correcting the dangling modifiers. Be sure to use a comma if necessary. If the sentence is correct as written, write *correct* in the space provided.

1. The stores will be crowded when shopping this weekend.

   _____

2. Having sent out your résumé, it is a good idea to follow up with a phone call.

   _____

3. Driving too fast on a residential road, police cars will be on the lookout.

   _____

4. Looking for a good used car, the local newspaper can sometimes be helpful.

   _____

5. Believing what the witness said to be true, the judge sentenced the defendant to three years' probation.

   _____

6. To be eligible for the contest, a certified letter is required.

   _____

7. With anger in her eyes, Marian slammed the door on her boyfriend.

   _____

8. Jean's office was cleaned out while on a business trip.

   _____

9. Eager to start his new job, the days seemed to go by slowly.

   _____

10. The paperwork can be completed while waiting to see the doctor.

   _____

**Answers are on page 132.**

# Renaming Phrases

Another type of modifying phrase is an **appositive,** or **renaming phrase.** Like all modifying phrases, a renaming phrase should be placed as closely as possible to the noun it renames. Use commas to separate the renaming phrase from the rest of the sentence.

Look at how you can combine two sentences by using commas and a renaming phrase:

Please give this report to Ms. Falcone. Ms. Falcone is our administrative team leader.

becomes

Please give this report to Ms. Falcone, our administrative team leader.

## EXERCISE 4

**Directions:** Combine the following pairs of sentences using renaming phrases. Be sure to place commas correctly.

1. Next year our tournament will be held in Westwood. Our tournament is the Amateur Chess League Championship.

   _____

2. The contract will be mailed to you before the end of the week. The contract is a final sales agreement.

   _____

3. Let me introduce to you Mr. Rick Sipe. Mr. Rick Sipe is the new sports information director.

   _____

4. Mike Gomez has been named Employee of the Month again. Mike Gomez is one of our most valuable team members.

   _____

5. Angela organized the volunteer supper program. Angela is my wife's sister.

   _____

6. The project will be ready for presentation once these final changes are made. The project is a product development timeline.

   _____

*Answers are on page 132.*

# Using Parallel Structure

Compound elements in a sentence should have the same form, or **parallel structure.**

**Incorrect:**   My strengths are intelligence, efficiency, and I am loyal.

**Correct:**   My strengths are intelligence, efficiency, and loyalty.

**EXERCISE 5**

**Directions:**   Rewrite each sentence below to correct the element that is not parallel.

1. Studies suggest that cutting back on red meat, using whole grains, and raw vegetables can reduce the risk of cancer.

   _____

2. When the weather is hot, you should drink lots of water, stay out of the sun, and avoiding strenuous exercise.

   _____

3. A planned agenda and having an organized leader are key elements for a good meeting.

   _____

4. When you are writing, do you spend more time drafting your piece or to revise it?

   _____

5. When test driving a new car, listen for irregular sounds and you should make sure the odometer reflects the correct mileage.

   _____

6. The new assistant was hired on Monday, began work on Tuesday, and she quit on Wednesday.

   _____

7. Your son is capable, kind, and being a fun kid.

   _____

8. To get the job done, we will have to work harder, stay later, and helping each other.

   _____

*Answers are on page 132.*

# Unclear Pronouns

A pronoun should clearly agree with its **antecedent** (the word it refers to in a sentence). On the Language Arts, Writing Test, you will be asked to identify and correct unclear pronouns. If there is no antecedent, you'll need to add one.

**Incorrect:**   Mrs. Andrews and Ms. Wong agreed to **her** proposal. *(Whose proposal?)*

**Correct:**   Mrs. Andrews and Ms. Wong agreed to **Ms. Wong's** proposal.

**Incorrect:**   **They** say people should reduce their intake of saturated fat. *(Who are they?)*

**Correct:**   **Nutritionists** say people should reduce their intake of saturated fat.

**EXERCISE 6**

**Directions:**   Rewrite each incorrect sentence below, getting rid of any unclear pronouns. If the sentence is correct as written, write *correct* on the line provided.

1. In the letter they say we'll be getting bonuses in July instead of January.

   _____

2. Mr. Davis gave John the report he wrote.

   _____

3. The boys brought their backpacks into the house.

   _____

4. They say you can get very sick from getting bitten by a rabid dog.

   _____

5. As she walked by the elderly woman, she looked up and smiled.

   _____

6. The secretary called the committee members to let them know about the change in meeting time.

   _____

7. Sarah reviewed the plans that Tammy drew, and she had to redraw them.

   _____

8. When my husband and I made this purchase, we were fully aware of the risks involved.

   _____

*Answers are on page 132.*

# Pronoun Agreement

A pronoun should agree with, or match, its antecedent in number and in person.

**Incorrect:** The **men** in the meeting kept raising **his** voice.

**Correct:** The **men** in the meeting kept raising **their** voices.

**Incorrect:** When **a person** accidentally hits a parked car, **you** should leave a note on the windshield.

**Correct:** When **a person** accidentally hits a parked car, **he or she** should leave a note on the windshield.

**EXERCISE 7**

**Directions:** For each sentence below, underline the pronoun that agrees with the antecedent. Circle the antecedent.

1. My aunt's stepsons brought *(his, their)* toys to the cookout.

2. Everyone should remember to bring *(his or her, their)* ideas to the next committee meeting.

3. When a girl becomes a teenager, *(she, they)* can get rebellious.

4. The company has frequently publicized *(its, their)* policy on sick leave and long-term disability.

5. Both my boss and his colleagues plan to bring *(his, their)* spouses to the dinner.

6. Volunteers should arrive by noon, and *(he or she, they)* will be assigned a workstation at that time.

7. When we read the classified ads, *(you, we)* could not believe how many different kinds of jobs there are.

8. One of the women on the trip wanted to get *(her, their)* program signed by the cast.

9. Nobody wants *(his, their)* beard shaved without *(his, their)* consent.

10. Neither the pianist nor the violinists brought *(her, their)* music along.

11. When someone works hard, *(you, they, he or she)* will succeed.

12. It's a good idea to wave to your neighbor now and then; *(he or she, they)* will appreciate it.

*Answers are on page 133.*

# Using Correct Language

**Directions:** Choose the <u>one best answer</u> to each question. Some of the sentences may contain errors. A few sentences, however, may be correct as written. Read the sentences carefully and then answer the questions based on them. For each question, choose the answer that would result in the most effective writing of the sentence or sentences.

*Questions 1–4 refer to the following policy statement.*

## Customer Privacy Policy

### (A)

(1) The safeguarding of customer information is taken very seriously at MidTown Mortgage Company. (2) We understand our obligation to keep your customer information secure and confidential. (3) From time to time, we do share information with companies that provide products or services that may be of benefit to you our customer. (4) When we share any such information with our affiliate companies, we place strict limits on how it can be used. (5) We are committed to the following practices:

### (B)

1. (6) **We collect only the information that is needed to serve you and run our business.** (7) The information we collect for your files is used primarily for identification purposes to protect customer accounts and guard against unauthorized access to them. (8) Matching consumers' needs with products and services, added savings or convenience can be offered. (9) Finally, the information we collect helps us to identify potential risks to MidTown Mortgage.

### (C)

2. (10) **We carefully limit and control how your information is shared.** (11) We do not disclose your personal data to anyone, except as outlined in this policy statement. (12) Information we might share includes application material such as marital status, income, or are you employed. (13) Also, disclosure of information we have received from a consumer reporting agency, such as a credit history, is permitted.

### (D)

3. (14) **We limit employee access to your information.** (15) All MidTown employees are bound by a code of conduct that makes them responsible for protecting the confidentiality of customers' financial information. (16) Anyone actively engaged in specified tasks is authorized to use their access to customer information only to serve you better.

1. **Sentence 3: From time to time, we do share information with companies that provide products or services that may be of benefit to you our customer.**

   What correction should be made to sentence 3?

   (1) change *we* to *you*
   (2) insert a comma after *companies*
   (3) insert a comma after *services*
   (4) change *you* to *we*
   (5) insert a comma after *you*

2. **Sentence 8: Matching consumers' needs with products and services, <u>added savings or convenience can be offered.</u>**

   Which is the best way to write the underlined portion of the text? If the original is the best way, choose option (1).

   (1) added savings or convenience can be offered
   (2) offering added savings or convenience
   (3) we can offer added savings or convenience
   (4) added savings, or convenience can be offered
   (5) added savings or convenience are offered

3. **Sentence 12: Information we might share includes application material such as <u>marital status, income, or are you employed.</u>**

   Which is the best way to write the underlined portion of the text? If the original is the best way, choose option (1).

   (1) marital status, income, or are you employed
   (2) marital status, income, or employment
   (3) marital status, how much is your income, and are you employed
   (4) marital status, income, and is he or she employed
   (5) marital status, income, and are they employed

4. **Sentence 16: Anyone actively engaged in specified tasks is authorized to use their access to customer information only in order to serve you better.**

   What correction should be made to sentence 16?

   (1) change *their* to *his or her*
   (2) change *their* to *its*
   (3) change *you* to *them*
   (4) change *you* to *him*
   (5) no correction is necessary

   *Answers are on page 133.*

# Cumulative Review

**Directions:** Choose the <u>one best answer</u> to each question. Some of the sentences may contain errors in organization, sentence structure, usage, and mechanics. A few sentences, however, may be correct as written. Read the sentences carefully and then answer the questions based on them. For each question, choose the answer that would result in the most effective writing of the sentence or sentences.

*Questions 1–8 refer to the following political flyer.*

## A Message from the Election Commission

### (A)

(1) Citizens of the Fourth Congressional District will be selecting a successor to Representative Cecelia Raymond at special elections to be held this fall. (2) Special primary elections will be held on September 5, and a general election will be held on October 15. (3) Being an important right and responsibility of citizenship, please mark these dates on your calendar.

### (B)

(4) A review of the records in our office the Tritown Election Commission reveals that you are now an enrolled member of the Democratic Party. (5) This enrollment does not require you to vote for the Democratic candidate in the special state primary. (6) However, unless you choose to change your enrollment before August 15, you will be eligible to receive only a Democratic Party ballot in this election. (7) No further action is required, if you wish to receive this Democratic Party ballot. (8) If, however, you wish to vote in the Republican, Libertarian, or Green Party primary, please follow the instructions in the next paragraph.

### (C)

(9) To change your enrollment status, you must complete the attached card and return it to our office before August 15. (10) August can be a very humid month in many parts of this country. (11) Or you may change your enrollment at the office of your city or town clerk whenever they are open. (12) Be sure to check off the box marked *Party Enrollment Change* in the upper right-hand corner of the card.

### (D)

(13) The Election Commission would also like to remind you of the following voting regulations. (14) To register to vote in this state, you must be a U.S. citizen.

### (E)

(15) You must also live in the state and being at least 18 years old by the next election. (16) The penalty for illegal registration is a fine of no more than $10,000 or imprisonment for no longer than five years, or both.

1. Sentence 2: **Special primary <u>elections will be held on September 5, and</u> a general election will be held on October 15.**

   Which is the best way to write the underlined portion of the text? If the original is the best way, choose option (1).

   (1) elections will be held on September 5, and
   (2) election's will be held on September 5, and
   (3) elections will be held on September 5 and
   (4) elections will be held on September 5,
   (5) elections will be held on September 5, although

2. Sentence 3: **<u>Being an important right and responsibility of citizenship,</u> please mark these dates on your calendar.**

   Which is the best way to write the underlined portion of the text? If the original is the best way, choose option (1).

   (1) Being an important right and responsibility of citizenship
   (2) Because you are a responsible citizen
   (3) Because voting is an important right and responsibility of citizenship
   (4) Even though voting is important
   (5) Citizenship is important, so

3. Sentence 4: **A review of the records in <u>our office the Tritown Election Commission reveals</u> that you are now an enrolled member of the Democratic Party.**

   Which is the best way to write the underlined portion of the text? If the original is the best way, choose option (1).

   (1) our office the Tritown Election Commission reveals
   (2) our office the Tritown Election Commission reveal
   (3) our office, the Tritown Election Commission, reveals
   (4) our office, the Tritown Election Commission reveals
   (5) our office the Tritown Election Commission will reveal

4. Sentence 7: **No further action is required, if you wish to receive this Democratic Party ballot.**

   What correction should be made to sentence 7?

   (1) remove the comma after *required*
   (2) replace *if* with *although*
   (3) replace *if* with *because*
   (4) replace *you* with *they*
   (5) no correction is necessary

5. Sentence 10: **August can be a very humid month in many parts of this country.**

   Which revision should be made to sentence 10 to improve paragraph C?

   (1) move sentence 10 to the beginning of paragraph C
   (2) move sentence 10 to follow sentence 11
   (3) move sentence 10 to the end of paragraph C
   (4) remove sentence 10
   (5) no revision is necessary

6. Sentence 11: **Or you may change your enrollment at the office of your city or town clerk whenever they are open.**

   What correction should be made to sentence 11?

   (1) replace *you* with *he*
   (2) replace *your enrollment* with *his enrollment*
   (3) replace *whenever* with *although*
   (4) replace *they are* with *it is*
   (5) no correction is necessary

7. Which revision would improve this piece of writing?

   (1) move sentences 13 and 14 to the beginning of paragraph C
   (2) move sentences 13 and 14 to follow sentence 9
   (3) move sentences 13 and 14 to follow sentence 16
   (4) move sentences 13 and 14 to the beginning of paragraph E
   (5) no revision is necessary

8. Sentence 15: **You must also <u>live in the state and being</u> at least 18 years old by the next election.**

   Which is the best way to write the underlined portion of the text? If the original is the best way, choose option (1).

   (1) live in the state and being
   (2) live in the state, and being
   (3) have lived in the state and being
   (4) live in the state and be
   (5) live in the state and been

*Questions 9–15 refer to the following instructional pamphlet.*

## How to Protect Against Electrical Power Surges

### (A)

(1) Many areas of the country are threatened with electrical power outages as well as "brownouts," which are the planned reduction of voltage by some utilities to ward off total power failure. (2) This fluctuation in power voltage can cause damage to household appliances and electrical equipment. (3) Unless you take some precautions to protect your equipment. (4) There is dozens of reasons for uneven power flow, including lightning strikes, bad weather, damaged power lines, and utility transmission problems.

### (B)

(5) In the normal household in the United State's, the standard voltage is 120 volts. (6) If voltage increases or decreases from this norm, there can be a problem. (7) A power spike be a very short burst of high voltage lasting a fraction of a second. (8) A power surge, which is a longer burst of high energy, can cause more substantial damage. (9) Even if increased power voltage doesn't immediately damage equipment, it may wear components down over time by putting extra strain on the electrical system. (10) A device called a surge protector is recommended to prevent this damage.

### (C)

(11) Surge protection is provided by two basic types of units. (12) The first is called a surge arrestor, which is a high-energy device installed near the point where wires enter the building. (13) These are often referred to as a "whole-house surge protector." (14) It requires a certified electrician for installation, and it is relatively expensive. (15) The other major type of surge protection is called a surge suppressor, which is a low-energy device installed near the equipment to be protected. (16) There are a number of models on the market, and they are not expensive. (17) Electrical engineers also recommends another kind of protection especially for computers. (18) An uninterrupted power supply system runs on batteries in case of power outages, and it gives you several minutes to shut down his computer before any damage occurs.

9. Sentences 2 and 3: **This fluctuation in power voltage can cause damage to household appliances and <u>electrical equipment. Unless you take</u> some precautions to protect your equipment.**

   Which is the best way to write the underlined portion of the text? If the original is the best way, choose option (1).

   (1) electrical equipment. Unless you take
   (2) electrical equipment. Unless he takes
   (3) electrical equipment, unless you take
   (4) electrical equipment unless you take
   (5) electrical equipment because you take

10. Sentence 4: **There is dozens of reasons for uneven power flow, including lightning strikes, bad weather, damaged power lines, and utility transmission problems.**

    What correction should be made to sentence 4?

    (1) replace *is* with *are*
    (2) replace *is* with *was*
    (3) remove the comma after *flow*
    (4) remove the comma after *strikes*
    (5) no correction is necessary

**11. Sentence 5:** **In the normal household in the United State's, the standard voltage is 120 volts.**

What correction should be made to sentence 5?

(1) insert a comma after *normal*
(2) change *State's* to *States*
(3) remove the comma after *State's*
(4) change *is* to *was*
(5) no correction is necessary

**12. Sentence 7:** **A power spike be a very short burst of high voltage lasting a fraction of a second.**

What correction should be made to sentence 7?

(1) change *be* to *had been*
(2) change *be* to *be*
(3) change *be* to *is*
(4) change *lasting* to *lasted*
(5) no correction is necessary

**13. Sentence 13:** **These are often referred to as a "whole-house surge protector."**

Which is the best way to write the underlined portion of the text? If the original is the best way, choose option (1).

(1) These are often referred
(2) These are often, referred
(3) These will be often referred
(4) This is often referred
(5) This are often referred

**14. Sentence 17:** **Electrical engineers also recommends another kind of protection especially for computers.**

What correction should be made to sentence 17?

(1) change *engineers* to *engineer's*
(2) change *recommends* to *recommending*
(3) change *recommends* to *recommend*
(4) change *computers* to *computer's*
(5) no correction is necessary

**15. Sentence 18:** **An uninterrupted power supply system runs on batteries in case of power outages, and it gives you several minutes to shut down his computer before any damage occurs.**

What correction should be made to sentence 18?

(1) change *runs* to *run*
(2) change *runs* to *ran*
(3) remove the comma after *outages*
(4) change *gives* to *give*
(5) replace *his* with *your*

*Answers are on page 133.*

# Mechanics

*Language Arts, Writing pages 177–195*
*Complete GED pages 135–152*

Capitalize proper nouns. **Proper nouns** are nouns that name a specific person, place, or thing.

**Incorrect:**   We knew that jack's Birthday was on may 12.

**Correct:**      We knew that **J**ack's **b**irthday was on **M**ay 12.

## EXERCISE 1

**Directions:**   Correct the capitalization errors in the sentences below.

1. Our new Cousin is named Madeleine Caviness, and she was born in china.

2. The manager of our sales department gave a speech at the annual Meeting.

3. Next sunday is greg goldsmith's retirement party, so all his former Employees are holding a dinner party in his honor.

4. The Spring is usually the busiest time of the year for Betty's Thrift Shoppe.

5. Jalil and Malik are this Year's honored Graduates at roxbury high school.

6. Did you buy that Fur on your trip to new york?

7. The delegates from both Countries arrived at the conference ready to learn from each other and negotiate fairly.

8. Her son needed to see a Doctor immediately, yet she was turned away from county hospital without any help whatsoever.

9. The refreshment committee made the decision to serve mexican food at the Banquet.

10. All State governments now have the right to set a speed limit of 65 miles per hour on rural interstate highways.

11. The Newspaper quoted mayor fay as saying she was in favor of the new gun legislation.

12. The administrative assistant sends all his photocopying to burns copy company because of its fast turnaround time.

13. Take a left onto Ash Hill road, and you will see our House on the left-hand side of the Street.

14. The autobiographer recalled that august was the month she found most relaxing.

*Answers are on page 133.*

# Homonyms

A **homonym** is a word that sounds the same as another word but is spelled differently. The spelling items on the GED Language Arts, Writing Test are commonly misspelled homonyms.

**Incorrect:** Its a decision that the committee made on it's own.

**Correct:** **It's** a decision that the committee made on **its** own.

**Incorrect:** Sonia felt confident that she had **past** the exam.

**Correct:** Sonia felt confident that she had **passed** the exam.

## EXERCISE 2

<u>Part A</u>     **Directions:** Underline the homonym in parentheses that will correctly complete each sentence below.

1.  The swimming instructor told her she was (two, to, too) young to be in the class.

2.  The family had perfect (weather, whether) during (its, it's) vacation out west this spring.

3.  Press your right foot firmly upon the vehicle (breaks, brakes) in order to come to a full stop.

4.  The older members brought (they're, there, their) mementos to the reunion, and (they're, their, there) excited to share them.

5.  When you are (threw, through) with the test, hand your booklet to the monitor.

6.  Whitney's Dream, the winning horse, (passed, past) Amos's Future in the last leg of the race.

<u>Part B</u>     **Directions:** Find and correct the spelling errors in the memo below.

TO:     All Residents
FROM:   Maureen Burns

Its time to review the resident policy for coffee brakes. People have been abusing they're privileges by not signing in or out and leaving to frequently. You no who you are. Please remember to right your name on the signout sheet so that supervisors know who is wear. If we go threw another weak like this passed one, we will be forced to limit breaks to specific times.

Thank you for your cooperation.

*Answers are on page 134.*

# Commas

The following five rules provide a quick review of how commas are used correctly in writing.

1.  Use a comma to separate more than two items in a series.

    Lisa made beef stew, baked potatoes, and pea salad.

2.  Use a comma after an introductory element.

    In his lifetime, he has seen three major wars.

3.  Use commas to separate an appositive from the rest of the sentence.

    Katie, a yellow Labrador retriever, lay quietly on the couch.

4.  Use a comma between independent clauses joined by a conjunction.

    She packed her bags, for it was time to go.

5.  Use a comma in a complex sentence when the dependent clause precedes the independent clause.

    Because his shift had ended, the doctor went home.

## EXERCISE 3

**Directions:** Correct the comma errors in the following sentences by crossing out unnecessary ones and inserting them when they are needed.

1. Benjamin Jones a construction worker takes dance classes in the evening.

2. My sister bought a plane ticket, and left yesterday.

3. Until the lawyer hears from the client no action will be taken.

4. Please consider giving up your seat, if an elderly person boards the train.

5. Wishing to remain anonymous the donor did not attend the ceremony.

6. Hamburgers, and hot dogs are on the cookout menu for tomorrow.

7. Frustration boredom and irritation are all manageable emotions.

8. The customers saw the china and they fell in love with it right away.

9. I would like to introduce Mary Jo our event photographer.

10. The time of the meeting, is eleven thirty in the morning.

*Answers are on page 134.*

# Mechanics

**Directions:** Choose the <u>one best answer</u> to each question. Some of the sentences may contain errors. A few, however, may be correct as written. Read the sentences carefully and then answer the questions based on them. For each question, choose the answer that would result in the most effective writing of the sentence or sentences.

*Questions 1–6 refer to the following article.*

## Risk Factors for Poor Stroke Recovery

**(A)**

(1) What does it take to recover well from the effects of a stroke? (2) Researchers in maryland have recently completed a study that may help to answer this question. (3) Most interesting in there findings is the idea that certain personality traits may actually speed recovery, while others may impede it.

**(B)**

(4) By interviewing the close relatives and caregivers of more than 30 stroke victims, the research team learned that some personality features wood allow patients to be more adaptive during recovery. (5) "People described as self-conscious or introverted were less likely to heal thoroughly and quickly," said one team member. (6) These people tended to get depressed and not follow post-stroke rehabilitation plans designed by their doctors. (7) On the other hand, people who were described by their caregivers as outgoing problem solvers recovered well, even though they suffered identical stroke-related debilities.

**(C)**

(8) This research could have an important impact on how medical personnel design rehabilitation plans for individual patients. (9) For example one recommendation is for a brief psychological examination within a few days after a patient suffers a stroke. (10) Such an exam could help to identify self-conscious versus outgoing personalities so that Hospital workers could tailor specific recovery plans.

1. Sentence 2: **Researchers in maryland have recently completed a study that may help to answer this question.**

   What correction should be made to sentence 2?

   (1) insert a comma after *Researchers*
   (2) change *maryland* to *Maryland*
   (3) change *study* to *Study*
   (4) insert a comma after *help*
   (5) no correction is necessary

2. Sentence 3: **Most interesting in there findings is the idea that certain personality traits may actually speed recovery, while others may impede it.**

   What correction should be made to sentence 3?

   (1) change *there* to *their*
   (2) change *there* to *they're*
   (3) insert a comma after *traits*
   (4) change *recovery* to *Recovery*
   (5) no correction is necessary

3.  Sentence 4: **By interviewing the close relatives and caregivers of more than 30 stroke victims, the research team learned that some personality features wood allow patients to be more adaptive during recovery.**

    What correction should be made to sentence 4?

    (1)  remove the comma after *victims*
    (2)  replace *some* with *sum*
    (3)  change *research* to *Research*
    (4)  replace *wood* with *would*
    (5)  insert a comma after *patients*

4.  Sentence 7: **On the other hand, people who were described by their caregivers as outgoing problem solvers recovered well, even though they suffered identical stroke-related debilities.**

    What correction should be made to sentence 7?

    (1)  remove the comma after *hand*
    (2)  replace *their* with *they're*
    (3)  insert a comma after *caregivers*
    (4)  remove the comma after *well*
    (5)  no correction is necessary

5.  Sentence 9: **For example one recommendation is for a brief psychological examination within a few days after a patient suffers a stroke.**

    What correction should be made to sentence 9?

    (1)  insert a comma after *example*
    (2)  insert a comma after *recommendation*
    (3)  change *psychological* to *Psychological*
    (4)  change *patient* to *Patient*
    (5)  no correction is necessary

6.  Sentence 10: **Such an exam could help to identify self-conscious versus outgoing personalities so that Hospital workers could tailor specific recovery plans.**

    What correction should be made to sentence 10?

    (1)  insert a comma after *help*
    (2)  change *Hospital* to *hospital*
    (3)  change *workers* to *Workers*
    (4)  insert a comma after *workers*
    (5)  no correction is necessary

    *Answers are on page 134.*

 Go to **www.GEDWriting.com** for additional practice and instruction!

# Cumulative Review

**Directions:** Choose the <u>one best answer</u> to each question. Some of the sentences may contain errors in organization, sentence structure, usage, and mechanics. A few sentences, however, may be correct as written. Read the sentences carefully and then answer the questions based on them. For each question, choose the answer that would result in the most effective writing of the sentence or sentences.

*Questions 1–8 refer to the following memo.*

TO:      All Med-Inc Employees
FROM:  Joseph Wilson

**(A)**

(1) As is customary at this time of year, I am writing to inform you of some changes that will take place in the three departments under my supervision. (2) This has been a fantastic year for Med-Inc, and we should congratulate each other on a job well done. (3) Of course, there are several things we can and should improve on, and it is the managements hope that the changes outlined below will help us achieve these improvements. (4) As you know, our company motto—We Can Change for the Better— is something I try to live up to each and every day I came to work.

**(B)**

(5) The change that will perhaps have the most impact on how we work together is the planned closing of the Hillsdale office. (6) Despite our efforts over the past three years to make this expansion a positive reality, the fact is that we are losing money there. (7) The office will close as of the first of next year, and the service department will move to the downtown location. (8) The good news is that there are no loss of jobs here; all Hillsdale employees will be relocated within the company.

**(C)**

(9) Sondra has worked at Med-Inc. for seven years, and she has consistently demonstrated leadership, integrity, and intelligence. (10) We have asked Sondra to lead the operations team in creating a new way to do business. (11) Please congratulate Ms. Bell. (12) When you see her in the hallways or in the cafeteria.

**(D)**

(13) Finally, I am pleased to announce our exciting new bonus and incentive program. (14) Under this program, each manager will have discretionary funds available to give special bonuses at any time of the year. (15) Seeing extraordinary hard work by someone, a check can be presented on the spot. (16) If a manager wants to reward an entire team for a job well done, funds are available for that too. (17) Please feel free to come to me, the personnel staff, or going to your supervisor if you have any questions about this new program.

1. Sentence 3: **Of course, there are several things we can and should improve on, and it is the managements hope that the changes outlined below will help us achieve these improvements.**

   What correction should be made to sentence 3?

   (1) remove the comma after *course*
   (2) change *are* to *is*
   (3) remove the comma after *on*
   (4) change *managements* to *management's*
   (5) replace *us* with *them*

2. Sentence 4: **As you know, our company motto—We Can Change for the Better—is something I try to live up to <u>each and every day I came to</u> work.**

   Which is the best way to write the underlined portion of the text? If the original is the best way, choose option (1).

   (1) each and every day I came to
   (2) each and every day I came too
   (3) each and every day I come to
   (4) each and every day, I came to
   (5) each and every Day I came to

3. Sentence 6: **Despite our efforts over the past three years to make this expansion a positive reality, the fact is that we are losing money there.**

   If you rewrote this sentence beginning with

   *The fact is that we are losing money there*

   the next word should be

   (1) even
   (2) so
   (3) for
   (4) but
   (5) if

4. Sentence 8: **The good news is that there are no loss of jobs here; all Hillsdale employees will be relocated within the company.**

   What correction should be made to sentence 8?

   (1) change *is* to *was*
   (2) change *there* to *they're*
   (3) change *are* to *is*
   (4) change *Hillsdale* to *hillsdale*
   (5) no correction is necessary

5. Which sentence below would be most effective at the beginning of paragraph C?

   (1) Med-Inc. will always be a leader in medical technology because it has strong roots in the industry.
   (2) The sales department needs some new leadership.
   (3) My next announcement relates to the new flextime plan that will enable all employees to set hours suitable to their personal lives.
   (4) My second major announcement is the promotion of Sondra Bell to the position of director of operations.
   (5) Unfortunately, Sondra Bell will no longer be working here at Med-Inc.

6. Sentences 11 and 12: **Please <u>congratulate Ms. Bell. When you see</u> her in the hallways or in the cafeteria.**

   Which is the best way to write the underlined portion of the text? If the original is the best way, choose option (1).

   (1) congratulate Ms. Bell. When you see
   (2) congratulate Ms. Bell, when you see
   (3) congratulate Ms. Bell when you see
   (4) congratulate Ms. Bell although you see
   (5) congratulate Ms. Bell so you see

7. Sentence 15: <u>Seeing</u> extraordinary hard work by someone, a check can be presented on the spot.

Which is the best way to write the underlined portion of the text? If the original is the best way, choose option (1).

(1) Seeing
(2) Having seen
(3) If you see
(4) If a manager sees
(5) See

8. Sentence 17: Please feel free to come to me, the personnel <u>staff, or going to your supervisor if</u> you have any questions about this new program.

Which is the best way to write the underlined portion of the text? If the original is the best way, choose option (1).

(1) staff, or going to your supervisor if
(2) staff or going to your supervisor if
(3) staff, or your supervisor if
(4) staff, or go to your supervisor if
(5) staff, or going to your supervisor, if

*Questions 9–15 refer to the following instructional pamphlet.*

### Understanding the Three Asthma Zones

**(A)**

(1) Asthma is a disease that causes the air passages in your lungs to swell or narrow, making it harder for you to breathe. (2) This difficulty in breathing can vary in severity depending on many factors, such as exposure to dust, mold animals, and cigarette smoke. (3) Other things that may bother people with asthma are aspirin, colds, dirty air, and expressions of emotion such as laughing and crying. (4) Therefore, your asthma can be worse at certain times of the day depending on you're environment.

**(B)**

(5) This pamphlet will help you understand the three levels of asthma care you may need during the course of the day. (6) Your care action plan involves using a device called a "peak flow meter" to measure how well your lungs are working. (7) To ensure the effectiveness of your asthma-care action plan, you should first determine your personal best peak flow. (8) To do this, measure your peak flow three times first thing every morning. (9) The highest reading is your current peak flow. (10) Measure your peak flow every day for two weeks, when your asthma is under control. (11) The highest number over this two-week period is your personal best peak flow. (12) The following information about the three asthma zones will help you determine which medicines you should be taking depending on your peak flow reading. (13) The green zone indicates that your current peak flow is more than 80 percent of your personal best. (14) At this level, you are probably feeling pretty good. (15) You probably need to use only the long-term control medicines indicated in your action plan. (16) Your asthma is in the yellow zone when your peak flow is between 50 and 79 percent of your personal best. (17) When you are in the yellow zone, you may feel short of breath, and you may be coughing or wheezing. (18) At this time, use special precautions and taken quick-relief medicines.

**(C)**

(19) When your current peak flow is less than 50 percent of your personal best, you have entered the red zone, which indicates an asthma attack. (20) Heart attacks are equally frightening. (21) You may be having trouble breathing and have pain in your chest. (22) You should seek help immediately at the nearest Clinic or emergency room.

9. Sentence 2: **This difficulty in breathing can vary in severity depending on many factors, such as exposure to dust, mold animals, and cigarette smoke.**

   What correction should be made to sentence 2?

   (1) change *This* to *These*
   (2) change *breathing* to *Breathing*
   (3) insert a comma after *mold*
   (4) change *cigarette* to *Cigarette*
   (5) no correction is necessary

10. Sentence 4: **Therefore, your asthma can be worse at certain times of the day depending on you're environment.**

    What correction should be made to sentence 4?

    (1) remove the comma after *Therefore*
    (2) change *times* to *time's*
    (3) insert a comma after *day*
    (4) change *you're* to *your*
    (5) no correction is necessary

11. Sentence 10: **Measure your peak flow every day for two <u>weeks, when your asthma is</u> under control.**

    Which is the best way to write the underlined portion of the text? If the original is the best way, choose option (1).

    (1) weeks, when your asthma is
    (2) weeks when your asthma is
    (3) weeks, so that your asthma is
    (4) weeks, but your asthma is
    (5) weeks, when your asthma was

12. Which revision would make paragraph B more effective?

    (1) begin a new paragraph with sentence 9
    (2) remove sentence 10
    (3) remove sentence 11
    (4) begin a new paragraph with sentence 12
    (5) no revision is necessary

13. Sentence 18: **At this time, use special precautions and taken quick-relief medicines.**

    What correction should be made to sentence 18?

    (1) remove the comma after *time*
    (2) change *use* to *using*
    (3) change *taken* to *take*
    (4) change *taken* to *took*
    (5) no correction is necessary

14. Sentence 20: **Heart attacks are equally frightening.**

    Which revision should be made to sentence 20?

    (1) remove sentence 20
    (2) move sentence 20 to the beginning of paragraph C
    (3) move sentence 20 to the end of paragraph B
    (4) move sentence 20 to follow sentence 18
    (5) move sentence 20 to follow sentence 21

15. Sentence 22: **You should seek help immediately at the nearest Clinic or emergency room.**

    What correction should be made to sentence 22?

    (1) replace *You* with *They*
    (2) replace *You* with *He*
    (3) change *Clinic* to *clinic*
    (4) change *emergency room* to *Emergency Room*
    (5) no correction is necessary

    ***Answers are on page 134.***

# Evaluate Your Progress

On the following chart, circle the number of any item you answered incorrectly in the Cumulative Review for each chapter. Next to each group of item numbers, you will see the pages you can review to learn how to answer the items correctly. Pay particular attention to areas where you missed half or more of the questions.

| Skill Area | Item Number | | | | | Review Pages (L and C) |
| --- | --- | --- | --- | --- | --- | --- |
| | pages (21–23) | pages (34–37) | pages (47–50) | pages (60–64) | pages (70–73) | |
| **ORGANIZATION** Text divisions | | | 5 | 7 | 12 | 120–126$^L$; 157–160$^C$ |
| Topic sentences | | | 13 | | 5 | 115–119$^L$ 153–157$^C$ |
| Unity/coherence | | | 7, 11 | 5 | 14 | 127–133$^L$ 160–165$^C$ |
| **SENTENCE STRUCTURE** Complete sentences, fragments, and sentence combining | | 11 | | 9 | 6 | 19–24, 83–104$^L$; 105–108, 110–112$^C$ |
| Run-on sentences/ comma splices | | 7 | 14 | | | 86–88, 96$^L$; 108–109$^C$ |
| Wordiness/repetition | | | | | | 97–98, 103–104$^L$; 116–121$^C$ |
| Coordination/subordination | | 13 | 6, 10 | | 3 | 83–84, 89–98$^L$; 116–118$^C$ |
| Modification | | | | 2 | 7 | 145–153$^L$; 126–128$^C$ |
| Parallelism | | | | 8 | 8 | 154–156$^L$; 129–134$^C$ |
| **USAGE** Subject-verb agreement | 3, 9, 11, 12 | 1, 3, 5, 10, 12 | 4, 12, 16 | 6, 10, 14 | 4 | 51–59, 62–73$^L$; 87–91$^C$ |
| Verb tense/form | 4, 6, 8, 10 | 8, 9 | 1, 3, 15 | 12 | 2, 13 | 51–61, 101–102$^L$; 73–86$^C$ |
| Pronoun reference/ antecedent agreement | 1, 5, 7 | | | 13, 15 | | 38–42, 157–165$^L$; 91–95$^C$ |
| **MECHANICS** Capitalization | | | | | 15 | 29, 34–35, 177–178$^L$; 135–138$^C$ |
| Punctuation (commas) | | 2 | 2, 8 | 1, 3, 4 | 9, 11 | 31, 87, 93, 96, 183–185$^L$; 139–144$^C$ |
| Spelling (possessives, contractions, and homonyms) | 2 | 4, 6 | 9 | 11 | 1, 10 | 43, 179–182$^L$; 147–149$^C$ |

$^L$Contemporary's GED Language Arts, Writing
$^C$Contemporary's Complete GED

# Preparing for the GED Essay

*Language Arts, Writing pages 207–218*
*Complete GED pages 169–196*

## What the GED Essay Is Like

**EXERCISE 1**

**Directions:** Read the following statements about the GED essay and decide if they are true or false. Write *T* or *F* on the appropriate line. If a statement is false, rewrite it correctly on the lines below.

_____ 1. You have one hour to write your GED essay.

_____ 2. You need a lot of specialized knowledge to write your GED essay.

_____ 3. If you receive a score below 2.0 on the essay, you have to take both parts of the GED Language Arts, Writing Test again.

_____ 4. Readers will mark every error on your paper and then count the number of errors to determine your score.

_____ 5. You have a choice of two questions when you write your essay.

_____

_____

_____

_____

_____

*Answers are on page 135.*

# The Writing Process

**EXERCISE 2**

**Directions:**  Number the steps of the writing process in order from 1 (*first*) to 4 (*last*) on the lines below.

_____  Writing

_____  Organizing

_____  Gathering ideas

_____  Revising

*Answers are on page 135.*

**EXERCISE 3**

**Directions:**  Circle the letter of the appropriate description for each step in the writing process.

1.  Writing

    a.  Make sure the essay is well written.

    b.  Write the introductory, body, and concluding paragraphs.

2.  Organizing

    a.  Get as many ideas down on paper as possible.

    b.  Put the ideas in an order that makes sense.

3.  Gathering ideas

    a.  Figure out the essay topic and think of ideas for the essay.

    b.  Write in complete sentences and paragraphs.

4.  Revising

    a.  Check the completed essay to make sure it is okay.

    b.  Check the idea list to make sure that all of the ideas are about the essay topic.

*Answers are on page 135.*

# The Five-Paragraph Essay

**EXERCISE 4**

**Directions:** Match each part of the five-paragraph essay with its appropriate description.

_____ 1. Introductory paragraph

_____ 2. Body paragraphs

_____ 3. Concluding paragraph

a. details and examples that back up the main idea of the essay

b. a restatement and summary of the main idea of the essay

c. an overview of the main idea of the essay

***Answers are on page 135.***

# Using the GED Scoring Guide to Improve Your Work

**EXERCISE 5**

**Directions:** Read the following essay topic and idea list. Then read the criteria from the GED Essay Scoring Guide. Circle the number that best describes the idea list.

————————— T O P I C —————————

Why do you want to get your GED?

In your essay, give your reasons for wanting to get your GED.
Explain the reasons for your choice.

*get a better job*
*make more money*
*feel better about myself*
*have my kids look up to me*

**Scoring criteria:**

**LEVEL 4** writing has specific and relevant details and examples.

**LEVEL 3** writing incorporates some focused, specific details.

**LEVEL 2** writing provides few specific details. Details may be limited to a listing, repetitions, or generalizations.

**LEVEL 1** writing lacks details or examples or presents irrelevant information.

***Answers are on page 135.***

# Gathering Your Ideas

*Language Arts, Writing pages 219–230*
*Complete GED pages 169–196*

## Analyzing the GED Essay Question

**EXERCISE 1**

**Directions:** Read the following GED essay topics. Write the topic of each question on the line and determine how you will respond. Check the appropriate box.

1. ———————————— T O P I C ————————————

   What are the characteristics of a good father?

   In your essay, describe the characteristics of a good father. Explain the reasons for your beliefs. Use your personal observations, experience, and knowledge.

   Topic: _____

   How will you respond?
   ☐ state an opinion
   ☐ state causes and effects
   ☐ compare and contrast

2. ———————————— T O P I C ————————————

   Which is more important to you—your career or your family?

   In your essay, state whether you believe your career or your family is more important. Explain the reasons for your views. Use your personal observations, experience, and knowledge.

   Topic: _____

   How will you respond?
   ☐ state an opinion
   ☐ state causes and effects
   ☐ compare and contrast

3. ———————————————— **T O P I C** ————————————

What is the biggest problem facing our country today?

In your essay, describe the biggest problem facing our country today. Explain the reasons for your opinion. Use your personal observations, experience, and knowledge.

Topic: _____

How will you respond?
- ☐ state an opinion
- ☐ state causes and effects
- ☐ compare and contrast

4. ———————————————— **T O P I C** ————————————

Many people put off until tomorrow things that they could do today.

Write an essay explaining why people procrastinate. Describe the possible results of this procrastination.

Topic: _____

How will you respond?
- ☐ state an opinion
- ☐ state causes and effects
- ☐ compare and contrast

5. ———————————————— **T O P I C** ————————————

What are the benefits of getting an education?

In your essay, explain the benefits of getting an education. Give specific examples. Use your personal observations, experience, and knowledge.

Topic: _____

How will you respond?
- ☐ state an opinion
- ☐ state causes and effects
- ☐ compare and contrast

*Answers are on page 135.*

# Choosing Your Main Idea

**EXERCISE 2**

**Directions:** Look again at the GED essay topics in Exercise 1. Write a possible main idea for each essay on the lines below.

1. What are the characteristics of a good father?

   Main idea: _____

   _____

   _____

2. Which is more important to you—your career or your family?

   Main idea: _____

   _____

   _____

3. What is the biggest problem facing our country today?

   Main idea: _____

   _____

   _____

4. Many people put off until tomorrow things that they could do today.

   Main idea: _____

   _____

   _____

5. What do you think is the value of getting an education?

   Main idea: _____

   _____

   _____

*Answers are on page 135.*

# Thinking of Ideas and Supporting Details

**EXERCISE 3**

**Directions:** Look again at the following GED essay topics from pages 78 and 79. Think about the topic, type of response, and main idea for each. Brainstorm a list of ideas for each topic and complete the idea lists below.

1. Which is more important to you—your career or your family?

   Ideas/Supporting details:

   _____

   _____

   _____

   _____

2. What is the biggest problem facing our country today?

   Ideas/Supporting details:

   _____

   _____

   _____

   _____

3. What do you think is the value of getting an education?

   Ideas/Supporting details:

   _____

   _____

   _____

   _____

*Answers are on page 136.*

# Gathering Your Ideas

**Part A**   **Directions:**   Look at the GED essay topic that follows. Answer the questions below.

────────────────────────── T O P I C ──────────────────────────

New forms of communication are making the world a smaller place and are changing relations among people.

Write an essay explaining some of the effects of new forms of communication on people's lives.

1. What is the topic?_____

2. How will you respond? Check the appropriate box.

   ☐ state an opinion
   ☐ state causes and effects
   ☐ compare and contrast

3. Gather ideas using an idea map.

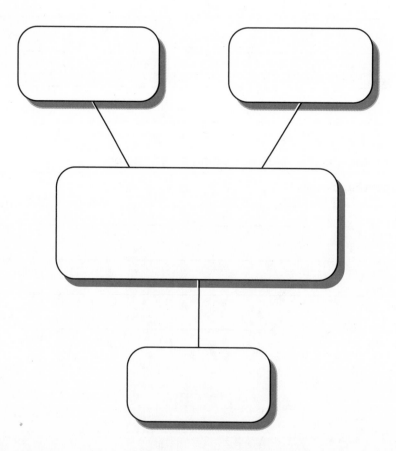

<u>**Part B**</u>    **Directions:**    Review the idea map you created in Part A and read the criteria on details from the GED Essay Scoring Guide. Circle the number of the score that best describes your idea map.

**Scoring criteria:**

<u>LEVEL</u> **4**    writing has specific and relevant details and examples.

<u>LEVEL</u> **3**    writing incorporates some focused, specific details.

<u>LEVEL</u> **2**    writing provides few specific details. Details may be limited to a listing, repetitions, or generalizations.

<u>LEVEL</u> **1**    writing lacks details or examples or presents irrelevant information.

<u>**Part C**</u>    **Directions:**    Now look again at your idea map. Add or cross off ideas to improve your score.

*Answers are on page 136.*

 Go to **www.GEDWriting.com** for additional practice and instruction!

# Organizing Your Ideas

*Language Arts, Writing pages 231–252*
*Complete GED pages 169–196*

## Deciding on a Pattern of Organization

**EXERCISE 1**

**Directions:** Read the following essay questions. Write the name of the appropriate pattern of organization *(time order, order of importance, cause and effect, or comparison and contrast)* on each line below.

_____ 1. What did you do on your last birthday?

_____ 2. Would you rather watch a movie at a local theater or wait to see the same movie on cable TV?

_____ 3. What caused you to return to school to get your GED?

_____ 4. What is your favorite TV show?

_____ 5. Would you rather own a cellular phone or a computer with high-speed Internet access?

_____ 6. Why are some people prejudiced against people of races, religions, or sexual orientations that are different from their own?

_____ 7. How do you and your family celebrate Thanksgiving Day?

_____ 8. What is your favorite style of clothing?

_____ 9. How do you get ready for work or school every morning?

_____ 10. If you won $1 million, what would you do with it?

**Answers are on page 136.**

# Arranging Your Ideas

**EXERCISE 2**

**Directions:** Look at the ideas one writer gathered for an essay on good places to shop and follow the instructions below.

Topic:                Good places to shop
How to respond:       Give reasons
Main idea:            Secondhand stores are good places to shop.

Ideas/Supporting details:
    wide selection
    many choices of style.
    no refunds or exchanges
    convenient
    located in many neighborhoods
    open the same hours as other stores
    low prices
    a complete outfit costs less than a new shirt
    good shoes cost $10 or less

1. Use circling to organize the ideas.

2. Cross off any ideas that do not belong.

3. Add an idea to any group that needs more ideas. Use brainstorming, the ideas already gathered, and the *wh*-questions to develop another idea.

4. Number the groups in the order in which you will write about them.

**Answers are on page 136.**

# Organizing Your Ideas

**Part A**  **Directions:**  Look at the ideas you gathered for the GED Practice Exercise on page 82 and answer the following questions.

1.  What pattern of organization will you use to organize your ideas? Circle your answer.

    time order
    order of importance
    cause and effect
    comparison and contrast

2.  Use circling, outlining, or making a chart to arrange your ideas. Cross off any irrelevant ideas.

3.  Make sure that your essay has enough ideas. Use brainstorming, the ideas you already gathered, and the *wh*-questions (*who? what? when? where? why?* and *how?*) to develop more ideas, if necessary.

4.  Number the groups in the order in which you will write about them.

**Part B**  **Directions:**  Look again at your organized ideas and read the criteria on organization from the GED Essay Scoring Guide. Circle the number of the description that best matches your organized list.

**Scoring criteria:**

LEVEL **4**  writing establishes a clear and logical organization.

LEVEL **3**  writing has an identifiable organizational plan.

LEVEL **2**  writing shows some evidence of an organizational plan.

LEVEL **1**  writing fails to display organized ideas.

**Part C**  **Directions:**  Now look at your organized ideas one more time. Find a way to improve the organization of your ideas in order to raise your score.

*Answers are on page 136.*

# Writing Your GED Essay

*Language Arts, Writing pages 253–270*
*Complete GED pages 169–196*

## Writing a Five-Paragraph Essay

**EXERCISE 1**

**Directions:** Circle the letter of the answer that correctly completes each statement below.

1. A good introductory paragraph

   a. is organized from specific to general.

   b. contains a thesis statement.

2. The thesis statement

   a. gives the main idea of the introductory paragraph.

   b. tells the reader what to expect in each body paragraph.

3. A good body paragraph

   a. begins with a topic sentence, a general statement of the paragraph's main idea.

   b. is very general and lacks detail.

4. A good body paragraph

   a. has support sentences that back up the main idea.

   b. restates the thesis statement.

5. A good concluding paragraph

   a. is organized from specific to general.

   b. gives a lot of specific detail.

*Answers are on page 136.*

## EXERCISE 2

<u>Part A</u>     **Directions:**     The paragraphs in the following five-paragraph essay are in the wrong order. Number them in the correct order from 1 *(first)* to 5 *(last)*.

a. ☐ _____

To sum up, the only thing better than eating one of these foods would be eating them all. To me, a perfect meal would start off with a nice leafy salad. Then I would have a slice or two of my favorite kind of pizza. And the perfect way to top it off would be with a couple of scoops of ice cream—different flavors, of course. Delicious!

b. ☐ _____

After salad, my next favorite food is pizza. I love almost any kind of pizza. I like thin crust, thick crust, and deep dish. I love to get a pizza with extra tomato sauce and extra cheese and piled with toppings like olives, onions, and broccoli. One of my favorite things to do is order a pizza on Friday night after a hard week at work. Then my husband and I sit back, relax, chat, watch TV, and enjoy a favorite meal.

c. ☐ _____

Of all my favorites, the only one that can beat out salad and pizza is ice cream. I love its cold sweetness. I especially like to eat ice cream at night right before bed. I also like to eat ice cream cones at the beach, and I love to serve my kids ice cream bars on picnics. The only problem is that I do not have one favorite flavor. I like mint chocolate chip, pistachio, and butter pecan. I also like fudge ripple and rocky road. In fact, I would be surprised to find a flavor I do not like!

d. ☐ _____

Everyone has favorite foods. Personally, I have always liked everything, so choosing one is hard. However, I could probably choose three. If I had to choose three favorite foods, I would have to say that my three favorites are salad, pizza, and ice cream.

e. ☐ _____

Of my three favorite foods, one is a crisp, cool salad. In the summer, a big salad of lettuce, tomatoes, and other greens is a refreshing treat. A salad is also good for my health. I always put in plenty of red and green peppers, which have lots of vitamin C. I like to add different kinds of lettuce, like red lettuce, which has some iron. Freshly sliced onions are also good for me, so I put in plenty of those.

<u>Part B</u>     **Directions:**     Look at the paragraphs again and write the appropriate label from the list below on the line above each paragraph. Make sure the paragraphs are numbered correctly.

Introductory paragraph
Body paragraph 1
Body paragraph 2
Body paragraph 3
Concluding paragraph

*Answers are on page 136.*

## GED PRACTICE
# Writing Your GED Essay

**Part A**     **Directions:**     Look at the idea list that you organized for the GED Practice Exercise on page 86. Use it to write a complete five-paragraph essay. The steps below will guide you through the essay-writing process.

1.  Look at the topic, main idea, and names of your groups. Use them to write an introductory paragraph on the lines below. Make sure that your introductory paragraph meets these characteristics:

  ☐ The paragraph is indented.
  ☐ The paragraph identifies the topic and main idea of the essay.
  ☐ The paragraph captures the reader's interest.
  ☐ The paragraph indicates the organization of the essay in the thesis statement.

_____

_____

_____

_____

_____

2.  Look at the three groups of ideas. Use them to write three body paragraphs on the lines below. Make sure that your body paragraphs meet these characteristics:

  ☐ The paragraphs are indented.
  ☐ The body paragraphs support, or back up, the thesis statement in the same order in which they are mentioned in the thesis statement.
  ☐ Each body paragraph begins with a topic sentence that is a complete sentence and indicates the main idea of that paragraph.
  ☐ The supporting sentences back up the topic sentence with more detailed information.

**Body Paragraph 1**

_____

_____

_____

_____

_____

**Body Paragraph 2**

_____

_____

_____

_____

_____

**Body Paragraph 3**

_____

_____

_____

_____

_____

3. Review your idea list and completed body paragraphs. Use them to write a concluding paragraph on the lines below. Make sure that your concluding paragraph meets these characteristics:

    ☐ The paragraph is indented.
    ☐ The concluding paragraph summarizes the information in the body paragraphs.
    ☐ The first sentence of the concluding paragraph rephrases the thesis statement.
    ☐ The other sentences relate the thesis statement to broader ideas.

_____

_____

_____

_____

_____

**Part B**     **Directions:**   Look at the five-paragraph essay you just wrote and read the criteria on development from the GED Essay Scoring Guide. Circle the number that best describes your five-paragraph essay.

Scoring criteria:

LEVEL **4**   writing achieves coherent development with specific and relevant details and examples.

LEVEL **3**   writing has focused but occasionally uneven development.

LEVEL **2**   writing has some development, but it may be limited to a listing, repetition, or generalizations.

LEVEL **1**   writing demonstrates little or no development.

**Part C**     **Directions:**   Look again at your essay. Find a way to improve the development of your essay in order to raise your score.

*Answers are on page 136.*

# Revising Your GED Essay

*Language Arts, Writing pages 271–296*
*Complete GED pages 169–196*

## Rating Your GED Essay

**EXERCISE 1**

**Directions:** Read the following GED essay topic and sample essay. Use the GED Essay Scoring Guide on page 93 to rate the essay.

---
### TOPIC
---

What is your favorite pastime?

In your essay, describe your favorite pastime. Explain the reasons for your choice. Use your personal observations, experience, and knowledge.

---

Everyone has a favorite pastime. I have three: I like to go to concerts, I like to go to church, and I like to eat out

I like to go to concerts. Last month I went to a really good concert. Elton John Played and Performed his songs. The concert really good. He playd the Piano and sang. He also showed a video of him with his friend Princess Diana.

Besides concerts, I like to go to Church. I like to sing in the choir and talk to my friends. Church is fun, but concerts more exciting.

I also like to eat out. My favorite food is fried chicken. I also like pizza and barbecue. When I eat out I feel relaxed because I dont' have to cook for my husband and kids. After the Elton John concert we went to the Fish Shop for some fried catfish.

Everyone needs a pastime. For me, concerts, church, and eating out are fun ways to spend time.

Score: _____

*Answers are on page 137.*

**LANGUAGE ARTS, WRITING, PART II**

# Essay Scoring Guide

|  | 1 | 2 | 3 | 4 |
|---|---|---|---|---|
|  | **Inadequate** | **Marginal** | **Adequate** | **Effective** |
| **Response to the Prompt** | **Reader has difficulty identifying or following the writer's ideas.** | **Reader occasionally has difficulty understanding or following the writer's ideas.** | **Reader understands the writer's ideas.** | **Reader understands and easily follows the writer's expression of ideas.** |
|  | Attempts to address prompt but with little or no success in establishing a focus. | Addresses the prompt, though the focus may shift. | Uses the writing prompt to establish a main idea. | Presents a clearly focused main idea that addresses the prompt. |
| **Organization** | Fails to organize ideas. | Shows some evidence of an organizational plan. | Uses an identifiable organizational plan. | Establishes a clear and logical organization. |
| **Development and Details** | Demonstrates little or no development; usually lacks details or examples or presents irrelevant information. | Has some development but lacks specific details; may be limited to a listing, repetitions, or generalizations. | Has focused but occasionally uneven development; incorporates some specific detail. | Achieves coherent development with specific and relevant details and examples. |
| **Conventions of EAE** | Exhibits minimal or no control of sentence structure and the conventions of Edited American English (EAE). | Demonstrates inconsistent control of sentence structure and the conventions of EAE. | Generally controls sentence structure and the conventions of EAE. | Consistently controls sentence structure and the conventions of EAE. |
| **Word Choice** | Exhibits weak and/or inappropriate words. | Exhibits a narrow range of word choice, often including inappropriate selections. | Exhibits appropriate word choice. | Exhibits varied and precise word choice. |

# Revising the Organization and Content

**EXERCISE 2**

**Directions:** Read the paragraph below. Revise the content and organization. Make sure the essay meets the criteria on the following list. Write your revised paragraph on the lines that follow.

Includes specific reasons to support the topic sentence
Includes specific examples
Includes specific details
Shows rather than tells
Includes transitions between sentences
Includes smooth wording with no repetition

    Many people prefer to shop over the Internet instead of going to the mall. You can buy almost anything on the Internet. You can buy the same things over the Internet as you can buy at the mall.

_____

_____

_____

_____

_____

_____

_____

_____

_____

_____

_____

_____

_____

**Answers are on page 137.**

# Checking for Edited American English

**EXERCISE 3**

**Directions:** Read the paragraph below. Check for errors in capitalization, sentence structure, subject-verb agreement, punctuation, and spelling. Use the following checklist, and make any necessary corrections.

---

**Checklist: Checking for Edited American English**

☐ Is the first word of every sentence capitalized?

☐ Are proper nouns capitalized?

☐ Are the sentences complete?

☐ Do subjects and verbs agree?

☐ Does every sentence end in a period?

☐ Are commas used correctly?

☐ Are all the words spelled correctly?

---

My best friend is my dog, abby. She is loyal cuddly and sweet. I love her very much, I don't know what I would do without her. Last month she got very sick, so I taked her to the vet. The vet said she has a tumor and needed an operashun. The operashion was very expensive but I saved up enough money for it. Her was very week after her surgery, so I took special care of her. Now she is almost back to her old self. Running around the backyard. Chasing birds. I am so reliefed that she got better.

***Answers are on page 137.***

# Revising Your GED Essay

**Part A**    **Directions:** Look at the essay that you wrote in the GED Practice Exercise on page 89. Use the GED Essay Scoring Guide on page 93 to give it a score. If possible, show your essay to your instructor or another student and have him or her score your essay, too.

Your score: _____    Other reader's score: _____

**Part B**    **Directions:** Revise the content and organization of your essay. Make your corrections directly on the essay. Use the checklist below as a revision guide.

---

### Checklist: Revising for Content and Organization

☐ Is there an introductory paragraph? Does it have a thesis statement?

☐ Are all the ideas relevant?

☐ Does each body paragraph have a topic sentence?

☐ Are the thesis statement and the body paragraphs in the same order?

☐ Does every body paragraph have two to three supporting ideas?

☐ Does the essay have specific reasons and examples?

☐ Does the essay show rather than tell, using specific details?

☐ Does the essay use sentence and paragraph transitions?

☐ Does the essay avoid repetition and wordiness?

---

**Part C**    **Directions:** Now revise your essay for Edited American English. Make your corrections directly on the essay. Use the checklist below as a revision guide.

---

### Checklist: Checking for Edited American English

☐ Is the first word of every sentence capitalized?

☐ Are proper nouns capitalized?

☐ Are the sentences complete?

☐ Do subjects and verbs agree?

☐ Does every sentence end in a period?

☐ Are commas used correctly?

☐ Are all the words spelled correctly?

<u>Part D</u>    **Directions:**    Look at your revised essay and use the GED Essay Scoring Guide on page 93 to give it a new score. If possible, show your essay to your instructor or another student and have him or her give it a new score too.

Your score: _____    Other reader's score: _____

<u>Part E</u>    **Directions:**    Has your score improved? How much? How did revising improve your score? Write a brief explanation on the lines below.

_____

_____

_____

_____

_____

*Answers are on page 137.*

 Go to **www.GEDWriting.com** for additional practice and instruction!

# Review of the Writing Process

## Writing a GED Essay

**Directions:** Follow the steps of the writing process to write a well-developed GED essay on the following topic.

---
**T O P I C**
---

People can do many things to improve their neighborhoods.

Write an essay explaining what you would do to improve your neighborhood, how you would do it, and how it would improve things in your neighborhood.

---

1. Plan your time. Decide how you will use your 45 minutes.

   Gather ideas: _____ to _____

   Organize: _____ to _____

   Write: _____ to _____

   Revise: _____ to _____

2. Now follow the steps of the writing process. Try to stick to your plan for using your time. If you take more than 45 minutes, mark the step you are working on when you run out of time. Then finish your essay. When you finish, take note of the time again. This will help you figure out how much more quickly you will have to work in order to complete your essay in 45 minutes during the GED Test.

### Gather Your Ideas

Figure out the essay topic, pattern of organization, and main idea. Complete the notes below.

Topic: _____

How to respond: _____

Main idea: _____

Gather ideas. Brainstorm or use an idea map. Complete your notes in the space below.

## Organize Your Ideas

Figure out how you will arrange your ideas using the pattern of organization you have chosen. Organize your ideas into three groups and name the groups. Use circling or outlining to organize your ideas. If you used an idea map to gather your ideas, then you just need to make sure that you have three groups and give them names. Make sure that all of your ideas are relevant and that you have two to three good ideas in each group.

## Write Your Essay

Use your notes on the essay topic and main idea to write the introductory paragraph and thesis statement. Use your organized groups of ideas to write the body paragraphs. Restate the thesis statement in the concluding paragraph. Relate the ideas in your essay to broader issues. Write your essay on a separate sheet of paper.

## *Revise Your Essay*

Revise the content and organization of your essay. Make your corrections directly on the essay. Use the following checklist.

---

**Checklist: Revising for Content and Organization**

☐ Is there an introductory paragraph? Does it have a thesis statement?

☐ Are all the ideas relevant?

☐ Does each body paragraph have a topic sentence?

☐ Are the thesis statement and the body paragraphs in the same order?

☐ Does every body paragraph have two to three supporting ideas?

☐ Does the essay have specific reasons and examples?

☐ Does the essay show rather than tell, using specific details?

☐ Does the essay use sentence and paragraph transitions?

☐ Does the essay avoid repetition and wordiness?

---

Revise for Edited American English. Make your corrections directly on the essay. Use the following checklist.

---

**Checklist: Checking for Edited American English**

☐ Is the first word of every sentence capitalized?

☐ Are proper nouns capitalized?

☐ Are the sentences complete?

☐ Do subjects and verbs agree?

☐ Does every sentence end in a period?

☐ Are commas used correctly?

☐ Are all the words spelled correctly?

---

Whenever you make a change, cross off what you do not want the reader to read. Use a caret (^) to indicate material that you want to add.

3. Look at your final corrected essay. Use the GED Essay Scoring Guide on page 93 to give it a score. If possible, show your essay to your instructor or another student and have him or her score your essay too.

Your score: _____   Other reader's score: _____

*Answers are on page 137.*

# Language Arts, Writing

## Part I

This practice test will give you an opportunity to evaluate your readiness for the GED Language Arts, Writing Test.

**Directions:** Choose the <u>one best answer</u> to each question. Some of the sentences may contain errors in organization, sentence structure, usage, and mechanics. A few sentences, however, may be correct as written. Read the sentences carefully and then answer the questions based on them. For each question, choose the answer that would result in the most effective writing of the sentence or sentences. You should take approximately 75 minutes to complete Part I.

**Practice Test Answer Grid**

| | | | |
|---|---|---|---|
| 1 ① ② ③ ④ ⑤ | 18 ① ② ③ ④ ⑤ | 35 ① ② ③ ④ ⑤ |
| 2 ① ② ③ ④ ⑤ | 19 ① ② ③ ④ ⑤ | 36 ① ② ③ ④ ⑤ |
| 3 ① ② ③ ④ ⑤ | 20 ① ② ③ ④ ⑤ | 37 ① ② ③ ④ ⑤ |
| 4 ① ② ③ ④ ⑤ | 21 ① ② ③ ④ ⑤ | 38 ① ② ③ ④ ⑤ |
| 5 ① ② ③ ④ ⑤ | 22 ① ② ③ ④ ⑤ | 39 ① ② ③ ④ ⑤ |
| 6 ① ② ③ ④ ⑤ | 23 ① ② ③ ④ ⑤ | 40 ① ② ③ ④ ⑤ |
| 7 ① ② ③ ④ ⑤ | 24 ① ② ③ ④ ⑤ | 41 ① ② ③ ④ ⑤ |
| 8 ① ② ③ ④ ⑤ | 25 ① ② ③ ④ ⑤ | 42 ① ② ③ ④ ⑤ |
| 9 ① ② ③ ④ ⑤ | 26 ① ② ③ ④ ⑤ | 43 ① ② ③ ④ ⑤ |
| 10 ① ② ③ ④ ⑤ | 27 ① ② ③ ④ ⑤ | 44 ① ② ③ ④ ⑤ |
| 11 ① ② ③ ④ ⑤ | 28 ① ② ③ ④ ⑤ | 45 ① ② ③ ④ ⑤ |
| 12 ① ② ③ ④ ⑤ | 29 ① ② ③ ④ ⑤ | 46 ① ② ③ ④ ⑤ |
| 13 ① ② ③ ④ ⑤ | 30 ① ② ③ ④ ⑤ | 47 ① ② ③ ④ ⑤ |
| 14 ① ② ③ ④ ⑤ | 31 ① ② ③ ④ ⑤ | 48 ① ② ③ ④ ⑤ |
| 15 ① ② ③ ④ ⑤ | 32 ① ② ③ ④ ⑤ | 49 ① ② ③ ④ ⑤ |
| 16 ① ② ③ ④ ⑤ | 33 ① ② ③ ④ ⑤ | 50 ① ② ③ ④ ⑤ |
| 17 ① ② ③ ④ ⑤ | 34 ① ② ③ ④ ⑤ | |

# PRACTICE TEST

*Questions 1–7 refer to the following brochure.*

### DuBois Early Childhood Center

**(A)**

(1)The DuBois Early Childhood Center is a facility that is friendly and doesn't cost much. (2) We have a specialized staff and a commitment to serving the entire community. (3) There are a variety of programs at the center for children at all developmental levels. (4) Our director, Nancy Updike, is a graduate of Southwestern University.

**(B)**

**Child Care:** (5) Childcare is available from 7 A.M. to 6 P.M. for infants toddlers and preschoolers. (6) This program is tuition-based, and the staff are all state licensed and certified.

**(C)**

**Preschool:** (7) We offer a half-day class to three- and four-year-olds. (8) Which focuses on helping children develop independence and social skills. (9) Basic prekindergarten skills are taught, but this is a play-centered program. (10) Tuition is $450 per month.

**(D)**

**School Readiness Program:** (11) This state-funded program for four-year-olds prepare them for kindergarten. (12) There is no cost for eligible families.

**(E)**

**Head Start:** (13) This is a free program for children ages three to four. (14) To qualify, a childs family must be at or below the national income poverty level.

**(F)**

(15) The mission of the DuBois Early Childhood Center is to provide individualized educational programs for children from birth to age six. (16) We serve Crete and the communities that surround it. (17) Our staff continually evaluates and improves the programs to better meet the needs of our children, what their families need, and help the community, too. (18) We promise that our preschool curriculum, coupled with parental support, will provide a solid foundation for future school success.

1. Sentence 1: **The DuBois Early Childhood Center is a facility that is friendly and doesn't cost much.**

   The most effective revision of sentence 1 would end with which group of words?

   (1) a facility that is friendly and doesn't cost much either.
   (2) a facility that is not costly or unfriendly.
   (3) a facility that is friendly and inexpensive.
   (4) a friendly and not very costly facility.
   (5) a facility both friendly and not costly.

2. Sentence 4: **Our director, Nancy Updike, is a graduate of Southwestern University.**

   Which revision should be made to sentence 4?

   (1) move sentence 4 to follow sentence 2
   (2) move sentence 4 to follow sentence 17
   (3) move sentence 4 to the end of the paragraph F
   (4) remove sentence 4
   (5) no revision is necessary

## PRACTICE TEST

3. Sentence 5: **Childcare is available from 7 a.m. to 6 p.m. for infants toddlers and preschoolers.**

   What correction should be made to sentence 5?

   (1) change *is* to *are*
   (2) change *from* to *between*
   (3) insert a comma after *6 P.M.*
   (4) insert commas after *infants* and *toddlers*
   (5) no correction is necessary

4. Sentences 7 and 8: **We offer a half-day class to three- and four-year-<u>olds. Which focuses on helping children</u> develop independence and social skills.**

   Which is the best way to write the underlined portion of the text? If the original is the best way, choose option (1).

   (1) -olds. Which focuses on helping children
   (2) -olds. Helping children
   (3) -olds, which focuses on helping children
   (4) -olds, it focuses on helping children
   (5) -olds. In which children are helped to

5. Sentence 11: **This state-funded program for four-year-olds <u>prepare them</u> for kindergarten.**

   Which is the best way to write the underlined portion of the text? If the original is the best way, choose option (1).

   (1) prepare them
   (2) prepare 'em
   (3) prepares them
   (4) prepared them
   (5) been preparing them

6. Sentence 14: **To qualify, a childs family must be at or below the national income poverty level.**

   What correction should be made to sentence 14?

   (1) remove the comma after *qualify*
   (2) change *childs* to *child's*
   (3) insert a comma after *family*
   (4) capitalize *national*
   (5) no correction is necessary

7. Sentence 17: **Our staff continually evaluates and improves the programs to better meet the needs of our children, what their families need, and help the community, too.**

   The most effective revision of sentence 17 would include which group of words?

   (1) children better, and what their families need, plus the community.
   (2) children. To give their families what they need. And help the community, too.
   (3) children, what their families need, and what the community needs, too.
   (4) children, with what their families need and helping the community.
   (5) children, their families, and the community.

*Questions 8–14 refer to the following instructions.*

### Making Sushi Maki

**(A)**

(1) Sushi masters take up to ten years to master their craft, but that doesn't mean you can't make sushi at home. (2) There are many inexpensive and easy sushi recipes, like the maki recipe below, and many of them don't contain raw fish.

**(B)**

(3) Sushi maki is rice and filler rolled in seaweed. (4) To make it, you will need four things:

    a filler of some sort
    a clean, damp cloth
    sushi rice (flavored with vinegar and sugar)
    nori (dry, roasted seaweed)

(5) Some common ones are cucumber, avocado, steamed mushrooms, steamed carrots, egg, cream cheese, and mayonnaise. (6) If you use raw fish, make sure it is less then 24 hours old. (7) Don't use freshwater fish. (8) It may contain harmful parasites.

**(C)**

(9) To form the maki, stretch your cloth out on the counter and put a sheet of nori on top. (10) Spread about three tablespoons of rice on the nori, leaving one or two inches of free space at each end. (11) In the center of the rice belongs the filling ingredients, which should be cut in strips. (12) Roll up the entire thing like a rug. (13) After each turn, squeeze the roll slightly to make it nice and tight, then move the cloth down so it doesn't get rolled up into the sushi. (14) The rolling should be continued until the end of the nori sheet is reached. (15) Then, use a sharp knife to slice your sushi into pieces half an inch thick. (16) Serve the slices with dipping sauce, soy sauce, and wasabi (japanese horseradish).

8. **Sentence 1: Sushi masters take up to ten years to master their craft, but that doesn't mean you can't make sushi at home.**

    Which is the best way to write the underlined portion of the text? If the original is the best way, choose option (1).

    (1) their craft, but that
    (2) there craft, but that
    (3) they're craft, but that
    (4) their craft but that
    (5) their craft but, that

9. **Sentence 5: Some common ones are cucumber, avocado, steamed mushrooms, steamed carrots, egg, cream cheese, and mayonnaise.**

    The most effective revision of sentence 5 would begin with which group of words?

    (1) The more common ones are
    (2) Some common fillers are
    (3) Some common ones is
    (4) Some are
    (5) no revision is necessary

10. Sentence 6: **If you use raw fish, make sure it is less then 24 hours old.**

What correction should be made to sentence 6?

(1) change *you use* to *your using*
(2) remove the comma after *fish*
(3) replace *less* with *fewer*
(4) change *then* to *than*
(5) change *hours* to *hour's*

11. Sentences 7 and 8: **Don't use freshwater fish. It may contain harmful parasites.**

The most effective combination of sentences 7 and 8 would include which group of words?

(1) Don't use freshwater fish containing
(2) Don't use freshwater fish to contain
(3) Don't use freshwater fish it may contain
(4) Don't use freshwater fish, and it may contain
(5) Don't use freshwater fish because it may contain

12. Sentence 11: **In the center of the rice belongs the filling ingredients, which should be cut in strips.**

The most effective revision of sentence 11 would include which group of words?

(1) belong the filling ingredients, which should be
(2) belonged the filling ingredients, which should be
(3) belongs the filling ingredients what should be
(4) belongs the filling ingredients, which should been
(5) belongs the filling ingredients, who should be

13. Sentence 14: **The rolling should be continued until the end of the nori sheet is reached.**

The most effective revision of sentence 14 would begin with which group of words?

(1) Continued until the end of the nori sheet is reached should be the
(2) Until reaching the end of the nori sheet, the rolling should be
(3) Rolling until the end of the nori sheet is reached, continue
(4) The rolling, until the end of the nori sheet is reached, should be
(5) Continue rolling until you reach the end of the

14. Sentence 16: **Serve the slices with dipping sauce, soy sauce, and wasabi (japanese horseradish).**

What correction should be made to sentence 16?

(1) insert *up* after *Serve*
(2) insert a comma after *with*
(3) capitalize *japanese*
(4) remove the parentheses
(5) no correction is necessary

## PRACTICE TEST

*Questions 15–20 refer to the following article.*

### Avoiding Lyme Disease

**(A)**

(1) Here's a warning for all you nature-lovers out there: Go ahead, commune with the Universe, but be aware that a hidden enemy may be lurking in the woods. (2) I speak of the tiny deer tick a creature that can be as small as the period at the end of this sentence. (3) Deer ticks aren't a problem in and of theirselves; however, if they bite you, they can pass on a nasty infection called Lyme disease.

**(B)**

(4) The earliest symptom of Lyme disease is a rash that appears around the bite. (5) Be forewarned, about half the people who get Lyme disease never notice the tick, so that rash may be your first sign that you've been bit. (6) The rash starts out as a red spot or bump then, over a period of days or weeks, it grows to become as large as six inches in diameter. (7) Often, a person will have fever, fatigue, headaches, mild neck stiffness, or joint pain along with the rash.

**(C)**

(8) After a few weeks, the rash may spread to other parts of the body. (9) People with spreading infections may have the headaches, fatigue, and pain that I mentioned earlier. (10) Once their infections are spreading, people with Lyme disease may also suffer from numbness, temporary paralysis, even meningitis (infection of fluid around the brain). (11) This is no disease to mess around with, folks! (12) If you notice symptoms, see a physician right away. (13) In its early stages, Lyme disease is easily treated with antibiotics. (14) If you wait to long, however, you could face long-term problems like arthritis, nerve damage, or swelling of the heart muscle. (15) So enjoy your days in the great outdoors, but take care. (16) We'd like to keep you healthy and happy!

15. Sentence 2: **I speak of the tiny deer tick** a creature that can be as small as the period at the end of this sentence.

    Which is the best way to write the underlined portion of the text? If the original is the best way, choose option (1).

    (1) I speak of the tiny deer tick a
    (2) I speak of the tiny deer tick, a
    (3) I speak of the tiny deer tick. A
    (4) I speak of the tiny Deer tick a
    (5) I speak, of the tiny deer tick a

16. Sentence 3: **Deer ticks aren't a problem in and of theirselves; however, if they bite you, they can pass on a nasty infection called Lyme disease.**

    What correction should be made to sentence 3?

    (1) change *aren't* to *weren't*
    (2) change *theirselves* to *themselves*
    (3) replace *however* with *because*
    (4) insert a comma after *infection*
    (5) no correction is necessary

17. Sentence 5: **Be forewarned, about half the people who get Lyme disease never notice the tick, so that rash may be your first sign that <u>you've been bit.</u>**

Which is the best way to write the underlined portion of the text? If the original is the best way, choose option (1).

(1) you've been bit.
(2) you been bit.
(3) you'd be bit.
(4) you are bit.
(5) you've been bitten.

18. Sentence 6: **The rash starts out as a red spot or <u>bump then, over</u> a period of days or weeks, it grows to become as large as six inches in diameter.**

Which is the best way to write the underlined portion of the text? If the original is the best way, choose option (1).

(1) bump then, over
(2) bump then, in time and over
(3) bump. Then, over
(4) bump, then, over
(5) bump over

19. Sentences 9 and 10: **People with spreading infections may have the headaches, fatigue, and pain that I mentioned earlier. Once their infections are spreading, people with Lyme disease may also suffer from numbness, temporary paralysis, even meningitis (infection of fluid around the brain).**

The most effective combination of sentences 9 and 10 would include which group of words?

(1) Along with the headaches, fatigue, and pain that I
(2) Either headaches, fatigue, pain, numbness, or temporary
(3) After having the headaches, fatigue, and pain that
(4) Headaches, fatigue, and pain will have people
(5) By having spreading infections, people will suffer from

20. Sentence 14: **If you wait to long, however, you could face long-term problems like arthritis, nerve damage, or swelling of the heart muscle.**

What correction should be made to sentence 14?

(1) replace *wait* with *weight*
(2) replace *to* with *too*
(3) remove the commas around *however*
(4) capitalize *arthritis*
(5) no correction is necessary

*Questions 21–27 refer to the following letter.*

Court Clerk
35th District Court
660 Lexington Road
Lanyier, MI 48170-1891

To Whom it May Concern:

**(A)**

(1) The attached ticket was issued to me on may 5 after I was hit making a left-hand turn. (2) I believe, that the accident occurred because of unclear street markings on Lilly Road near its intersection with Warren.

**(B)**

(3) There are no white lines at that intersection. (4) To me, it looks as if there is only two lanes of traffic, one lane in each direction. (5) Most of the time, traffic moves through the intersection in two lanes. (6) That suggests that other people had the same impression. (7) Apparently we are all mistaken, there are two marked lanes and two invisible ones.

**(C)**

(8) At the time of my accident, traffic was moving in only two lanes, and one lane had stopped to allow me to turn. (9) The other lane was clear, and there was no traffic in it, so I assumed it was safe to cross. (10) However, a car slipped out of the motionless lane of traffic and hit me. (11) According to the investigating officer, that car was moving in an unmarked, but legal, inside lane. (12) I don't think the officer treated me with much respect. (13) Please consider painting in white lines to make the intersection less confusing and dangerous.

Sincerely,

Larry Estevez

21. **Sentence 1: The attached ticket was issued to me on may 5 after I was hit making a left-hand turn.**

    What correction should be made to sentence 1?

    (1) change *me* to *myself*
    (2) capitalize *may*
    (3) start a new sentence with *after*
    (4) start a new sentence with *making*
    (5) no correction is necessary

22. **Sentence 2: I believe, that the accident occurred because of unclear street markings on Lilly Road near its intersection with Warren.**

    What correction should be made to sentence 2?

    (1) remove the comma after *believe*
    (2) start a new sentence with *because*
    (3) start a new sentence with *near*
    (4) change *its* to *it's*
    (5) replace *with* with *on*

# PRACTICE TEST

**23. Sentence 4: To me, <u>it looks as if there is</u> only two lanes of traffic, one lane in each direction.**

Which is the best way to write the underlined portion of the text? If the original is the best way, choose option (1).

(1)  it looks as if there is
(2)  it looked as if there is
(3)  it look as if there is
(4)  it looks as if there was
(5)  it looks as if there are

**24. Sentence 6: That <u>suggests that other people had</u> the same impression.**

Which is the best way to write the underlined portion of the text? If the original is the best way, choose option (1).

(1)  suggests that other people had
(2)  suggest that other people had
(3)  suggests that other people has
(4)  suggests that other people have
(5)  suggests that other people must of had

**25. Sentence 7: Apparently <u>we are all mistaken, there are</u> two marked lanes and two invisible ones.**

Which is the best way to write the underlined portion of the text? If the original is the best way, choose option (1).

(1)  we are all mistaken, there are
(2)  we are all mistaken. There are
(3)  mistaken is what we all are, there are
(4)  being mistaken, there are
(5)  we are all mistaken and wrong, there are

**26. Sentence 9: <u>The other lane was clear, and there was no traffic in it,</u> so I assumed it was safe to cross.**

Which is the best way to write the underlined portion of the text? If the original is the best way, choose option (1).

(1)  The other lane was clear, and there was no traffic in it,
(2)  The other lane was clear,
(3)  With no traffic in it, the other lane was clear,
(4)  Being clear, there was no traffic in the other lane,
(5)  Clear and with no traffic in it was the other lane,

**27. Sentence 12: I don't think the officer treated me with much respect.**

Which revision should be made to sentence 12?

(1)  move sentence 12 to follow sentence 1
(2)  move sentence 12 to follow sentence 10
(3)  remove sentence 12
(4)  move sentence 12 to the end of the letter
(5)  no revision is necessary

*Questions 28–33 refer to the following article.*

**(A)**

(1) Do you avoid generic products? (2) Do you ever buy things you don't need just because they are on sale? (3) Do you ever shop just for the fun of it?

**(B)**

(4) If you answered yes to these questions you're probably not a tightwad, but don't pat yourself on the back just yet. (5) There's a growing movement of people in the United States who are proud to call themselves tightwads. (6) Members use Web sites and newsletters to share ideas on how to save money. (7) Having just moved into a new apartment, the suggestions on these Web sites were surprisingly appealing.

**(C)**

(8) If you really want to go out to eat, go out for lunch instead of dinner. (9) The experience is just as nice, but the prices are much lower.

**(D)**

(10) And never order drinks. (11) Order water and ask for a lemon slice to dress it up.

**(E)**

(12) When you cook, make enough for several meals and freeze it. (13) If you have food on hand, you'll go out to eat less often, and bulk cooking saves a lot of time. (14) A popular book called *Living in the real world* claims you can do a whole month's worth of cooking in just one day.

**(F)**

(15) Never shop for groceries when you're hungry. (16) If you do, you'll make lots of expensive and unhealthy impulse purchases. (17) Then, every few months, skip your trip to the grocery store entirely. (18) That way, you'll be forced to use up the extra food in your cabinets.

28. Sentence 4: **If you answered yes <u>to these questions you're</u> probably not a tightwad, but don't pat yourself on the back just yet.**

    Which is the best way to write the underlined portion of the text? If the original is the best way, choose option (1).

    (1) to these questions you're
    (2) to these questions. You're
    (3) too these questions you're
    (4) to these questions your
    (5) to these questions, you're

29. Sentence 7: **Having just moved into a new apartment, the suggestions on these Web sites were surprisingly appealing.**

    What correction should be made to sentence 7?

    (1) change *new* to *knew*
    (2) insert *I found that* before *the suggestions*
    (3) start a new sentence with *the suggestions*
    (4) change *these* to *them*
    (5) change *were* to *was*

# PRACTICE TEST

**30.** Which sentence below would be the most effective at the end of paragraph B?

(1) Here are some of my favorites.
(2) Money is really tight right now.
(3) I spend way too much on food.
(4) Most people think tightwads are a bad thing.
(5) Some people make fun of others for buying store brands.

**31. Sentence 14:** **A popular book called *Living in the real world* claims you can do a whole month's worth of cooking in just one day.**

What correction should be made to sentence 14?

(1) capitalize *real world*
(2) insert a comma after *claims*
(3) start a new sentence with *you can*
(4) change *whole* to *hole*
(5) change *month's* to *months*

**32. Sentences 15 and 16:** **Never shop for groceries when you're hungry. If you do, you'll make lots of expensive and unhealthy impulse purchases.**

The most effective combination of sentences 15 and 16 would include which group of words?

(1) when you're hungry by making lots of
(2) when you're hungry instead of making lots of
(3) when you're hungry, and if you do anyway you'll make lots of
(4) when you're hungry, or you'll make lots of
(5) when you're hungry to make lots of

**33.** Which revision would make the article more effective?

(1) begin a new paragraph with sentence 5
(2) combine paragraphs C and D
(3) begin a new paragraph with sentence 14
(4) combine paragraphs E and F
(5) remove sentence 18

# PRACTICE TEST

*Questions 34–39 refer to the following memo.*

TO:      Cashiers
FROM:  Bill Graham
RE:      Detecting Forged Bills

**(A)**

(1) All cashiers at valushop should know how to identify forged bills. (2) Its rare that we come across one, but forgery is becoming easier all the time thanks to new, improved copy machines. (3) The federal government has taken a number of steps to make valid bills easy to identify. (4) Make a point of doing one of the following spot checks on every bill you handle.

**(B)**

(5) You can run a counterfeit detector pen over a corner of the bill. (6) It left a black or brown mark on forged bills and a yellow mark on valid bills. (7) These pens are available in the office.

**(C)**

(8) In the background, you can look for fine lines. (9) This type of fine printing tends to blur when it is copied.

**(D)**

(10) Newer 20-dollar bills and 50-dollar bills have a numeral in two-tone ink. (11) The ink should look green when viewed from one angle and black when viewed from another. (12) Also, if you hold the newer bills up to the light, you see a hidden portrait to one side. (13) This is called a watermark, and it don't reproduce well.

**34. Sentence 1: All cashiers at valushop should know how to identify forged bills.**

What correction should be made to sentence 1?

(1) replace *at* with *of*
(2) capitalize *valushop*
(3) change *should know* to *should be knowing*
(4) insert a comma after *know*
(5) no correction is necessary

**35. Sentence 2: Its rare that we come across one, but forgery is becoming easier all the time thanks to new, improved copy machines.**

What correction should be made to sentence 2?

(1) change *Its* to *It's*
(2) replace *that* with *what*
(3) remove the comma after *one*
(4) start a new sentence with *thanks*
(5) remove the comma after *new*

36. Sentence 3: **The federal government has taken a number of steps to make valid bills easy to identify.**

The most effective revision of sentence 3 would include which group of words?

(1) If the federal government
(2) Because the federal government
(3) Usually the federal government
(4) For example, the federal government
(5) Fortunately, the federal government

37. Sentence 6: **It left a black or brown mark on forged bills and a yellow mark on valid bills.**

Which is the best way to write the underlined portion of the text? If the original is the best way, choose option (1).

(1) It left a
(2) It will leave a
(3) It had left a
(4) It will have left a
(5) It did leave a

38. Sentence 8: **In the background, you can look for fine lines.**

The most effective revision of sentence 8 would include which group of words?

(1) for fine lines in the background of the portrait.
(2) in the background you can try.
(3) in the background for fine lines looking.
(4) can be tried in the background.
(5) by you, in the background.

39. Sentence 13: **This is called a watermark, and it don't reproduce well.**

What correction should be made to sentence 13?

(1) remove the comma after *watermark*
(2) replace *and* with *but*
(3) replace *it* with *a watermark*
(4) change *don't* to *doesn't*
(5) replace *well* with *good*

# PRACTICE TEST

*Questions 40–44 refer to the following article.*

## Watch Out! Someone May Be Reading Your E-Mail!

**(A)**

(1) The things you produce at work belong to your company, and that includes e-mail messages. (2) Managers may read it at any time, for any reason. (3) They don't even have to get your permission or give you advance notice. (4) In fact, they have the right to show your e-mail to others.

**(B)**

(5) Obviously, most managers aren't taking the time to read through all of their employees' personal e-mail; it's just not worth the effort. (6) However, managers often review e-mail when there are problems with a particular employee or looking for ways to improve customer service. (7) It happens more often than people think. (8) What can you do to protect yourself? (9) Be careful what you write. (10) Don't use e-mail to discuss sensitive matters, like plans to leave your job. (11) When you talk to your doctor, do it in person or over the phone. (12) And don't be fooled into thinking you can write anything as long as you deleted the message afterward. (13) In many companies, e-mail is automatically saved without the knowledge of employees. (14) If that's the case at your company, every e-mail message you've ever written may be on file, even if you've deleted it from your personal records.

40. Sentence 2: **Managers may read it at any time, for any reason.**

    What correction should be made to sentence 2?

    (1) change *Managers* to *Manager's*
    (2) change *it* to *them*
    (3) move *at any time* to follow *may*
    (4) start a new sentence with *for any*
    (5) no correction is necessary

41. Which sentence below would be most effective at the beginning of paragraph A?

    (1) Twenty years ago, few people used e-mail.
    (2) Many Americans own computers.
    (3) E-mail makes it easier to keep in touch.
    (4) There are more threats to personal privacy today than ever before.
    (5) Most people think that the e-mail they send at work is private, but it isn't.

42. Which revision would make the article more effective?

    (1) combine paragraphs A and B
    (2) remove sentence 5
    (3) start a new paragraph with sentence 8
    (4) remove sentence 12
    (5) start a new paragraph with sentence 13

43. Sentence 6: **However, managers often review e-mail when there are problems with a particular employee <u>or looking</u> for ways to improve customer service.**

    Which is the best way to write the underlined portion of the text? If the original is the best way, choose option (1).

    (1) or looking
    (2) looking
    (3) by looking
    (4) or look
    (5) or when they are looking

44. Sentence 12: **And don't be fooled into thinking you can write anything as long as <u>you deleted</u> the message afterward.**

    Which is the best way to write the underlined portion of the text? If the original is the best way, choose option (1).

    (1) you deleted
    (2) you deletes
    (3) you delete
    (4) your deleting
    (5) you have deleted

## PRACTICE TEST

*Questions 45–50 refer to the following article.*

### Study Finds Cigarettes and Alcohol in Children's Films

#### (A)

(1) Most animated films show characters smoking or drinking. (2) Them are the findings of a recent study at the University of North Carolina. (3) More than 50 animated films that were released over the past 60 years were viewed by the researchers. (4) Sixty-eight percent showed at least one character who smoked or drunk. (5) Researchers looked for messages about the long-term effects of cigarettes and alcohol. (6) They found none. (7) Not even any implied messages. (8) The good guys in these films were just as likely to smoke or drink as the bad guys. (9) Pinocchio and Dumbo is good examples. (10) One smokes a cigar, and the other gets drunk.

#### (B)

(11) Representatives of the film industry objected to the study's findings. (12) They claim that the films portray these activities as unwholesome. (13) To be fair, the study does not show whether the films actually make children more likely to use tobacco or alcohol. (14) Nevertheless, it points out how important it is for parents to monitor what their children watch. (15) If you have children, keep an eye on what he watches.

---

45. Sentence 2: **Them are the findings of a recent study at the University of North Carolina.**

    What correction should be made to sentence 2?

    (1) change *Them* to *Those*
    (2) change *are* to *is*
    (3) insert a comma after *study*
    (4) do not capitalize *North*
    (5) no correction is necessary

46. Sentence 3: **More than 50 animated films that were released over the past 60 years were viewed by the researchers.**

    The most effective revision of sentence 3 would begin with which group of words?

    (1) The researchers viewed
    (2) Over the past 60 years and more than
    (3) What was viewed by the researchers were
    (4) More than 50 animated films over 60 years
    (5) By the researchers were viewed more than

47. Sentence 4: **Sixty-eight percent showed at least one character who <u>smoked or drunk.</u>**

    Which is the best way to write the underlined portion of the text? If the original is the best way, choose option (1).

    (1) who smoked or drunk.
    (2) what smoked or drunk.
    (3) which smoked or drunk.
    (4) who smoked or drank.
    (5) who smoked or drinked.

48. Sentence 7: **<u>Not even any implied messages.</u>**

    Which is the best way to write the underlined portion of the text? If the original is the best way, choose option (1).

    (1) Not even any implied messages.
    (2) Not any implied messages even.
    (3) No implied messages even.
    (4) There weren't even any implied messages.
    (5) Implied messages, none.

**49. Sentence 9: Pinocchio and Dumbo <u>is good examples.</u>**

Which is the best way to write the underlined portion of the text? If the original is the best way, choose option (1).

(1) is good examples.
(2) was good examples.
(3) has been good examples.
(4) been good examples.
(5) are good examples.

**50. Sentence 15: If you have children, keep an eye on what he watches.**

What correction should be made to sentence 15?

(1) change *If you have children,* to *Having children,*
(2) change *have* to *has*
(3) remove the comma
(4) change *he watches* to *they watch*
(5) no correction is necessary

*Answers are on page 119.*

# PRACTICE TEST

## *Essay Directions and Topic*

Look at the box on the following page. In the box is your assigned topic.

You must write on the assigned topic ONLY.

You will have 45 minutes to write on your assigned essay topic. You may return to the multiple-choice section after you complete your essay if you have time remaining in this test period.

Pay attention to the following features as you write:

- Well-focused main points
- Clear organization
- Specific development of your ideas
- Control of sentence structure, punctuation, grammar, word choice, and spelling

As you write be sure to do the following:

- Do not leave pages blank.
- Write legibly **in ink.**
- Write on the assigned topic.
- Write your essay on a separate sheet of paper.

---
TOPIC
---

Do you think that the minimum wage should be raised?

In your essay, state whether you believe the minimum wage should be raised. Explain your beliefs. Use your personal observations, experience, and knowledge.

---

Part II is a test to determine how well you can use written language to explain your ideas.

In preparing your essay, you should take the following steps:

- Read the **DIRECTIONS** and the **TOPIC** carefully.

- Plan your essay before you write. Use scratch paper to make any notes.

- After you finish writing your essay, reread what you have written and make any changes that will improve your essay.

Your essay should be long enough to develop the topic adequately.

**Evaluation guidelines are on page 122.**

# PRACTICE TEST
# Answer Key

**1.** (3) The new sentence is written parallel form: *friendly and inexpensive.*

**2.** (4) This brochure tells what the DuBois Early Childhood Center has to offer. Sentence 4 doesn't provide information on that topic, so it doesn't belong.

**3.** (4) Always separate three or more items in a series with commas: *infants, toddlers,* and *preschoolers.*

**4.** (3) Sentence 8 is a fragment; it has no subject, so it should be attached to the previous sentence.

**5.** (3) The subject of the verb *prepare* is *this state-funded program. Program* is a singular noun, so it should be paired with a singular verb: *prepares.*

**6.** (2) An apostrophe should be added to *childs* to show that the family belongs to the child.

**7.** (5) The three items in this series should be in the same form. Choice (5) does this by making each item a noun preceded by an adjective.

**8.** (1) This sentence is correct as written.

**9.** (2) In the original sentence it is unclear what *ones* refers to. Choice (2) makes it clear that the foods listed are possible fillers.

**10.** (4) *Then* is used to show that one event happened after another. *Than* is used in comparisons such as *less than.*

**11.** (5) The word *because* correctly shows that the second part of the sentence is the reason for the first.

**12.** (1) This sentence is turned around so that the subject appears after the verb. Its subject is *the filling ingredients.* Since *ingredients* refers to several things, the plural form of the verb should be used: *belong.*

**13.** (5) Choice (5) makes the sentence less wordy by eliminating the passive voice (*you reach* instead of *is reached*).

**14.** (3) Words that refer to particular countries should be capitalized, even when they are adjectives (describing words).

**15.** (2) The phrase beginning with *a creature* is a renaming phrase, so it should be set off with commas.

**16.** (2) *Theirselves* is not a word. The correct pronoun is *themselves.*

**17.** (5) After the helping verbs *have been,* you should use the *-ed* or *-en* form of a verb. In this case, it's *bitten.*

**18.** (3) The original sentence is a run-on. Choice (3) correctly separates the thoughts into two sentences.

**19.** (1) The symptoms in sentence 9 can appear at the same time as the symptoms in sentence 10. The linking phrase *along with* correctly expresses that relationship.

**20.** (2) *Too* refers to more than enough of something. *To* is a simple preposition.

**21.** (2) The names of months are proper nouns and should be capitalized.

**22.** (1) This comma separates the verb (*believe*) from its object (*that the accident occurred*). These two parts of the sentence belong together.

**23.** (5) When the subject of a verb is *there,* the verb should agree with the noun that follows it, in this case with *two lanes. Lanes* is plural, so the plural verb *are* should be used.

**24.** (4) This paragraph is in present tense (with the verbs *are, looks,* and *moves*), so the present tense verbs *suggests* and *have* should be used.

**25.** (2) The original sentence contains two thoughts separated by only a comma, creating a run-on sentence. Choice (2) correctly separates the thoughts into separate sentences.

**26.** (2) The original sentence contains two phrases that say the same thing: *was clear* and *there was no traffic in it.* It's best to cut out one phrase.

**27.** (3) This letter is about how the lanes on Lilly Road are marked. The officer's treatment of the writer has nothing to do with that topic, so sentence 12 doesn't belong.

**28.** (5) The phrase *if you answered yes to these questions* isn't part of the main sentence. It is an introductory clause, so it should be set off with a comma.

**29.** (2) The original sentence contains a dangling modifier. Choice (2) corrects the error.

## PRACTICE TEST

**30.** (1) This sentence works particularly well because it ties paragraph A to the list that follows it. Without choice (1), it's not immediately clear why the list is included in this article.

**31.** (1) In the titles of books, capitalize everything but minor words such as *the* and *in*.

**32.** (4) The word *or* correctly shows that readers can either avoid shopping when hungry or make impulse purchases.

**33.** (2) Paragraphs B and C are both about how to save money at restaurants, so they belong together.

**34.** (2) *Valushop* should be capitalized because it's the proper name of a particular store.

**35.** (1) Substitute *it is* for *its* in the sentence. *It is rare* makes sense, so the contraction *it's* is needed.

**36.** (5) Sentence 3 describes a solution to the problem discussed in sentence 2. The word *fortunately* correctly expresses this relationship.

**37.** (2) This paragraph is discussing actions that will be taken in the future, so the future tense (*will leave*) should be used.

**38.** (1) In the original sentence, *in the background* seems to describe where *you* should look. Choice (1) makes the correct meaning clear by moving the phrase away from *you* and specifying where the lines may be found.

**39.** (4) *Don't* should be used only after plural subjects or *I*. *It* is not plural, so it should be followed by *doesn't*.

**40.** (2) The word *it* is a substitute for *e-mail messages*. *E-mail messages* refers to several things, so *them* should be used.

**41.** (5) This option would be a great opening sentence for this article. It grabs the reader's interest by pointing out that something he or she probably believes really isn't true.

**42.** (3) Sentences 5–7 are about why and when managers read e-mail. Sentences 8–14 are about how to protect your privacy. The two sections break nicely into different paragraphs.

**43.** (5) In the original sentence, it is unclear who is looking for ways to improve customer service. Choice (5) makes it clear that the managers are.

**44.** (3) You cannot write a message in the present and delete it in the past. *Deleted* should be changed to *delete* so it is in the same tense as *can write*.

**45.** (1) The object pronoun *Them* should never be used as the subject of a verb.

**46.** (1) The original sentence seems to ramble because it doesn't tell you who it is about until the end. The new sentence moves this information to the beginning of the sentence: *the researchers viewed*.

**47.** (4) The past tense form of *drink* is *drank*. *Drunk* should be used only after a helping verb.

**48.** (4) All the choices except (4) are sentence fragments. Choice (4) correctly adds a subject (*there*) and a verb (*weren't*) to the original fragment.

**49.** (5) *Pinocchio* and *Dumbo* are two things, so they should be followed by a plural verb: *are*.

**50.** (4) The pronoun in this sentence is a substitute for *children*. *Children* refers to several people, so the plural pronoun *they* should be used.

# Part I: Evaluation Chart

On the following chart, circle the number of any item you answered incorrectly. For those questions that you missed, review the skill pages indicated. Pay particular attention to areas in which you missed half or more of the questions.

| Skill Area | Item Number | Review Pages in *Contemporary's GED Language Arts, Writing* | Review Pages in *Contemporary's Complete GED* |
|---|---|---|---|
| **ORGANIZATION** | | | |
| Text divisions | 33, 44 | 120–126 | 157–160 |
| Topic sentences | 41 | 115–119 | 153–157 |
| Unity/coherence | 2, 27, 30, 36 | 127–133 | 160–165 |
| **SENTENCE STRUCTURE** | | | |
| Complete sentences, fragments, and sentence combining | 4, 11, 32, 48 | 19–24, 83–104 | 105–108, 110–112 |
| Run-on sentences/ comma splices | 18, 25 | 86–88, 96 | 108–109 |
| Wordiness/repetition | 13, 19, 26, 46 | 97–98, 103–104 | 116–121 |
| Coordination/ subordination | | 83–84, 89–98 | 116–118 |
| Modification | 29, 38 | 145–153 | 126–128 |
| Parallelism | 1, 7, 42 | 154–156 | 129–134 |
| **USAGE** | | | |
| Subject-verb agreement | 5, 12, 23, 49 | 51–59, 62–73 | 87–91 |
| Verb tense/form | 17, 24, 37, 39, 43, 47 | 51–61, 101–102 | 73–86 |
| Pronoun reference/ antecedent agreement | 9, 16, 40, 45, 50 | 38–42, 157–165 | 91–95 |
| **MECHANICS** | | | |
| Capitalization | 14, 21, 31, 34 | 29, 34–35, 177–178 | 135–138 |
| Punctuation (commas) | 3, 8, 15, 22, 28 | 31, 87, 93, 96, 183–185 | 139–144 |
| Spelling (possessives, contractions, and homonyms) | 6, 10, 20, 35 | 43, 179–182 | 147–149 |

# Part II: Evaluation Guidelines

If possible, have your instructor or another student score your essay using the GED Essay Scoring Guide on page 93. If this is not possible, let your paper sit for a few days and then score it yourself.

After your essay has been scored, review your work using the following questions:

1. After you read your topic, did you plan your answer, jotting down ideas for your essay? Was this process easy or hard? If gathering your ideas seemed hard, review Chapter 9 in *Contemporary's GED Language Arts, Writing* or pages 170–175 in *Contemporary's Complete GED*.

2. Did you take time to organize your ideas before you began writing? Was this process easy or hard? For help on organizing your ideas, review Chapter 10 in *Contemporary's GED Language Arts, Writing* or pages 170–175 in *Contemporary's Complete GED*.

3. Were you able to write a clear introduction to your essay? Did the introduction clearly indicate the organization of the rest of the essay? For more information on this aspect of writing, review Chapter 11, pages 255–258, in *Contemporary's GED Language Arts, Writing* or pages 184–185 in *Contemporary's Complete GED*.

4. As you were writing your essay, were you able to compose body paragraphs that stated main ideas and supported them with plenty of details. For a review of this aspect of writing, see Chapter 11, pages 259–264, in *Contemporary's GED Language Arts, Writing* or pages 185–186 in *Contemporary's Complete GED*.

5. Were you able to write a clear concluding paragraph for your essay? For review in this area, see Chapter 11, pages 265–266, in *Contemporary's GED Language Arts, Writing* or page 186 in *Contemporary's Complete GED*.

6. After you finished writing, did you revise your essay to improve its content and organization? If you want to review this area, see Chapter 12, pages 276–292, in *Contemporary's GED Language Arts, Writing* or pages 193–195 in *Contemporary's Complete GED*.

7. After you finished writing, did you revise your essay to improve its control of spelling, punctuation, and so on? If you want to review this area, see Chapter 12, pages 293–294, in *Contemporary's GED Language Arts, Writing* or pages 193–195 in *Contemporary's Complete GED*.

# Additional Essay Topics

Use these topics for additional practice prior to the test. Remember to follow all the steps of the writing process to develop strong five-paragraph essays. Time your work so that you finish in 45 minutes. Use the GED Essay Scoring Guide on page 93 to evaluate your work.

---
**TOPIC 1**

What is your favorite pastime?

In your essay, describe your favorite pastime. Explain the reasons for your choice. Use your personal observations, experience, and knowledge.

---
**TOPIC 2**

Do people eat too much junk food?

In your essay, state whether you think people eat too much junk food. Explain your opinion. Use your personal observations, experience, and knowledge.

---
**TOPIC 3**

Should companies provide childcare for their employees' children?

In your essay, state whether you think companies should provide childcare options. Explain your opinion. Use your personal observations, experience, and knowledge.

---
**TOPIC 4**

Healthcare experts believe that a widespread lack of exercise is resulting in increasing health problems.

Write an essay in which you describe the effects of a lack of exercise.

---

# Answer Key

## Sentence Basics

**Exercise 1, page 1**

**Part A**

1. F; complete thought
2. F; subject
3. S
4. S
5. F; subject

**Part B**

**Paragraph with fragments:**

All employees should arrive at the meeting before nine o'clock tomorrow morning. **Important to be on time because we have a lot of issues to discuss.** Please be sure to tell your supervisor. **If you know you are going to be late.**

Most of the meeting will be focused on the new regulations on worker's compensation. **Thought it would be wise to provide adequate information about this extremely complex issue.**

**Corrected paragraph:**

All employees should arrive at the meeting before nine o'clock tomorrow morning. **It is** important to be on time because we have a lot of issues to discuss. Please be sure to tell your **supervisor if** you know you are going to be late.

Most of the meeting will be focused on the new regulations on worker's compensation. **We** thought it would be wise to provide adequate information about this extremely complex issue.

**Exercise 2, page 2**

1. woman; will help
2. singing; provides
3. sign; will be
4. members; plant
5. we; wanted
6. supervisors and workers; will be asked
7. signatures; are listed
8. people; marched
9. layer; lies
10. chaperoning; is required
11. waiters; deserve
12. discussion; followed

**Exercise 3, page 3**

1. you; did put
2. [you]; do not begin
3. [you]; reject
4. reasons; are
5. workers; did walk
6. customers; were waiting
7. officer; did arrive
8. confusion; seems
9. [you]; speak
10. game; will begin
11. everyone; will sit and listen
12. person; will be

**Exercise 4, page 4**

1. man's
2. stories
3. women's
4. workers'
5. family's
6. months
7. son's
8. taxes
9. parent's
10. employees

**Exercise 5, page 5**
**Part A**

1. me, him, her, us, them
2. He, She
3. your, his, her, their
4. he, she
5. our
6. Whose

**Part B**

1. ours
2. her
3. yours
4. them

**Exercise 6, page 6**
**Part A**

1. she
2. he
3. them

4. He
5. I
6. they
7. me
8. he
9. me
10. her; me

**Part B**

The staff and <u>I</u> would like to let you know that we are unhappy with your new lateness policy. <u>**Your**</u> ideas about improving performance are good, but the methods you plan to use are not fair to <u>**us.**</u>

You should not punish people the first time <u>**they**</u> are late. Instead, maybe you should send a report to the supervisor or <u>**her**</u> assistant. Then, if an employee is late again, you could tell <u>**him**</u> or <u>**her**</u> that he or she is on probation.

Please tell your boss, Mr. Wayne, to trust your employees to make <u>**their**</u> own decisions about arrival at work. If you and <u>**he**</u> punish too quickly, people may begin not to trust you or <u>**him**</u>.

**GED Practice, page 7**

1. (4) The possessive *person's* is correct here: *person's disease.*
2. (4) The original sentence is missing a verb to go with the subject of the clause, *steps.* Choice (4) corrects this error.
3. (2) The plural noun *ways* is correct here, not the possessive *way's.*
4. (4) The pronoun *they* is incorrect; use the possessive *their,* as in *their local community college.*
5. (3) The possessive *your* is correct here.
6. (3) The original version is a sentence fragment; choice (3) correctly uses the verb *use* as part of a command: *(you) use.*
7. (4) The compound pronoun *you* and *she* is the subject of the verb *traveled.*
8. (5) The plural *ideas* is correct here.

# Using Verbs

**Exercise 1, page 9**

1. saves, saved, will save
2. will graduate
3. were thinking, thought
4. will be

5. will work, will be working
6. called
7. will go, will be going
8. takes, took, will take
9. will see, will be seeing
10. plant, planted, will plant

**Exercise 2, page 10**

1. will have fired
2. has sold
3. have borrowed
4. had built
5. has reviewed
6. has learned
7. will have restored
8. had promised
9. had claimed
10. has input

**Exercise 3, page 11**

**Part A**

1. have gone
2. brought
3. was
4. had found
5. had run
6. was
7. had risen
8. won
9. had seen
10. have had

**Part B**

1. Record in the logbook any problems you **have seen** during any shift.
2. Be specific about what time the incident **took** place and who **was** involved.
3. Ask your shift partner to verify what you have recorded.
4. When you **have done** all of the above, sign your report and place it in your supervisor's mailbox.

**Exercise 4, page 12**

1. A federal survey published yesterday announced that the rate of violent crime in the United States fell for the sixth year in a row. The Bureau of Justice Statistics said that the number of rapes, assaults, and robberies was reduced by 15 percent during the year 2000. In addition, the report stated, property crimes **fell**

by 10 percent during the last year. However, critics of the survey stated that these statistics **apply** only to reported crime and that many violent crimes are not reported each year.

2. The following guidelines are designed to help you find the information you need to receive unemployment benefits.

    a. If you are under age 21, you need to call 1-800-555-1212 and ask for Form 27A.

    b. If you are over age 65, you **need** to report to the Senior Services Department at 123 North Street and show your ID and social security information.

    c. All other applicants **report** to Employment Services, also at 123 North Street.

3. Here are just some of the benefits you will receive if you open a Customer One account with us today. You **will receive** free checking for six months if you maintain a minimum balance of just $500. You will have the opportunity to do all your banking online with our easy new BankLink program. In addition, you **will be** able to take advantage of our low-interest loans with no money down. Sign up now and receive a free phone card worth $25!

4. Before you sign any contract or agreement with a home improvement company, make sure you know what you **will get** in return for your money. Unfortunately, there are many unlicensed con artists out there who are very skilled at duping unsuspecting consumers. For example, last year, one such con man signed up 300 customers for new heating systems that the homes did not even need. By the time the trick was discovered, the criminal "home improvement specialist" **was** long gone.

## Exercise 5, page 13

### Part A

1. weren't
2. doesn't
3. tell, are
4. bike
5. are
6. think, are
7. seems
8. states, am
9. is
10. do, are

### Part B

I **am** writing to inquire about an order I placed on November 1 of last year. The order number **is** #213980, and it was for a box of 12 votive candles. The candles **are** part of the Serenity Collection.

Although I have waited the suggested four weeks for delivery, I still **do not** have my order. This **does** not seem right. Will you please check on my order and let me know when I can expect delivery?

Your company has always provided me with excellent products and service. I **look** forward to doing more business with you in the future.

## Exercise 6, page 14

### Part A

1. plan
2. are
3. am
4. need
5. have
6. have
7. are
8. don't
9. are
10. is

### Part B

I called your office yesterday, and your secretary suggested that I write you a letter and enclose my résumé. She **believes** you are planning to do some hiring over the next several months, and I am very interested in working for your company.

My experience in clothing **has** been widespread, as you will see from my enclosed résumé. I worked for several years in a tailor's shop, mending and altering both men's and women's clothing. And, for the past two years, both my day job and my evening job **show** me that my future is in fashion. During the day, I **am** involved in matching customers with attractive styles at Dresses and More in the mall. At night, I work at Style Plus Factory, inspecting fabrics. Both these current jobs and my past experience **are** a good indication of my skills and interests.

I am looking forward to hearing from you soon, Ms. Kensington. As for my references, either my current employers or Mr. Chang **is** available at the phone numbers listed on my résumé.

Thank you for your time.

## Exercise 7, page 16

**Part A**
1. does (cook)
2. tell (you)
3. are (explanations)
4. is (doctor)
5. do (we)
6. were (forms)
7. come (you)
8. do (chairs); is (room)
9. sit (colleagues)
10. goes (friend)

**Part B**

A company spokesperson is expected to announce today that Castle Camera Company plans to lay off 100 more workers within the next month. This figure represents approximately one-quarter of the company's entire workforce. Neither employees nor company president Maureen Burns **was** available for comment.

Castle Camera, founded in 1925, **is** a major employer in this region, and the job loss is considered a major blow to the local economy. "There **is** no silver lining in this announcement," said Mayor Esther Hauser.

## Exercise 8, page 17

**Part A**
1. look
2. was
3. is
4. seems
5. have
6. is
7. are
8. has
9. are
10. thinks

**Part B**

I'm writing just to tell you that I, along with Joanna, **miss** working with you at Coffee Plus. Your bright smile and cheerful personality **are** sorely needed around here. In addition, the work you used to do in transcriptions **was** first rate, and no one can take your place!

Do you enjoy your new office? I know your decision to leave the people here **was** difficult. But you probably have lots of new friends and an easier pace and climate in which to work. I heard that three other people in your office **are** also former Coffee Plus employees!

## Exercise 9, page 18

1. is (either)
2. appear (most)
3. were (all)
4. was (all)
5. do (several)
6. looks (nothing)
7. receives (anyone)
8. do (few)
9. was (anything)
10. was (everything)
11. gets (everyone)
12. walk (both)
13. goes (no one)
14. are (some)
15. is (some)

## GED Practice, page 19

1. (3) The subject of the sentence is *policies*, not *handbook*, so the verb *are* is correct.
2. (3) The subject of the sentence is *rules and regulations*, so the verb should be plural.
3. (2) The indefinite pronoun *all* is plural in this sentence, so the verb *have* agrees with the subject, *all areas.*
4. (4) The verb of the sentence must agree with the subject closest to it, which in this case is *coworker.*
5. (5) The subject of the sentence is *space*, not *lines.* Therefore, the correct verb is singular: *space is.*
6. (1) Because the conjunction is *or*, not *and*, the subject of the sentence is singular: *socializing is.*
7. (2) The subject of the sentence is singular: *drinking is.*
8. (4) Do not be confused by the interrupting phrase *in addition to*; the subject of the sentence is singular, *grease*, which agrees with the verb *is.*
9. (3) The subject of the sentence is *consultant*, not *shifts*, so use a verb that agrees with a singular subject.

**Cumulative GED Practice, page 21**

1. (4) The possessive pronoun *your* is correct.
2. (4) The plural noun *lives* makes sense in this sentence, not the possessive.
3. (4) The subject of the sentence is plural: *some dangers are.*
4. (3) The original text is a sentence fragment. Changing the verb to *make* corrects the error.
5. (5) Use the object pronouns *him and her,* not the subject pronouns *he and she.*
6. (3) The correct past tense of the irregular verb *make* is *made.*
7. (2) The compound subject should include the subject pronoun *he,* not the object pronoun *him.*
8. (4) To form the present perfect tense, use *arrived,* not *arrive.*
9. (2) Since the subject of the sentence is singular, *building,* the correct verb form is *has been sold.*
10. (1) The passage is written in the present tense, so the future *will be* is not correct. The present tense *is* is correct.
11. (2) The indefinite pronoun *everyone,* not the plural *apartments,* is the subject of this sentence, so the verb *is* is correct.
12. (4) Because the conjunction is *nor,* not *and,* the verb should agree with the subject closer to it: *son deserves.*

# Combining Sentences

**Exercise 1, page 24**

**Part A**

1. It was a beautiful day outside, but the man carried his umbrella anyway.
2. The store has closed for the day, so all employees can punch out and go.
3. She is studying for the real estate license exam, so she can become a real estate agent.
4. We would love to hire a candidate like this one, for he would fit in well here.
5. You can pick up an application at the bank, or you can have an application mailed to you.
6. I am qualified for the job posted, and I would like to apply for it.

**Part B**

1. (1) This sentence does not join two independent clauses.
   **Corrected sentence:** The administrative assistant answers phones, and she does all typing.
2. Correct
3. (3) This sentence does not have a comma before the conjunction.
   **Corrected sentence:** Your order has been received, and it will be shipped on Wednesday.
4. (1) This sentence does not join two independent clauses.
   **Corrected sentence:** She was writing a letter home, but she forgot to mail it.
5. (2) This sentence does not use a conjunction that makes sense.
   **Corrected sentence:** The floors are covered with dog hair and shoe marks, so they look dirty.
6. Correct
7. (3) This sentence does not have a comma before the conjunction.
   **Corrected sentence:** The bonus in his paycheck was a surprise, and he appreciated it greatly.
8. (2) This sentence does not use a conjunction that makes sense.
   **Corrected sentence:** The printer is out of paper, so I will add more.
9. (1) This sentence does not join two independent clauses.
   **Corrected sentence:** The landscaper surveyed the yard, and he recommended weed control.
10. (3) This sentence does not have a comma before the conjunction.
    **Corrected sentence:** The book has just been published, and the author is on a sales tour.

**Exercise 2, page 26**

1. Our weekend dishwasher did not show up for work, **so** the night manager has to fill in.
2. Please let us know what size hotel room you will be needing, **and** decide what your arrival and departure dates will be.
3. The sales report indicates another successful quarter, **so** this is good news considering how much we have invested.

4. I enjoyed the presentation, **and** the film was also excellent and informative.
5. Correct
6. The package was shipped via overnight mail, **so** it should arrive before noon tomorrow.
7. Juanita schedules all employee vacations, **and** her assistant Fred distributes the information.
8. Correct
9. Tanya wrote the pages, **and** Samuel edited them.
10. Football is his favorite spectator sport, **but** he hates to actually play it.

## Exercise 3, page 27

### Part A

**Sample answers:**
1. Although the phone rang, no one answered it.
2. You will eat dinner with us each night because you are living in our house.
3. You are allowed to have up to three telephones since you have signed up for Family Plan Plus.
4. Bessie signed the enclosed documents although she did not agree with the terms stated.
5. My assistant will make the necessary corrections if there are some mistakes.
6. While Manuel was looking for a job, his wife could not leave the house.
7. He asked for the check when we finished our meal.
8. The new offices look really sharp even though the renovation was not expensive.
9. Because Sue asked for raises for her entire department, we saw an extra $20–$30 in our paychecks last month.
10. When my father arrives at home, he is surrounded by four screaming children.

### Part B

When you change your place of **employment, you** may be in the position of wondering what to do with the money you have accumulated in your retirement account. One option is to "roll over" the money into a new retirement **account so that** you will not have to pay taxes on that money. Or **if** you prefer, you can withdraw the money in one lump sum and pay taxes on it. Taking the lump sum also might require you to pay a "premature withdrawal" penalty of up to 10 percent.

It is always a good idea to consult with a tax **advisor before** you make any financial decisions of this magnitude. You have worked hard to earn this **money, so** you should take good care of it.

## Exercise 4, page 29

1. Please be sure to punch **in when** you arrive at the job site. We are finding that some employees are not punching in until after their first break. This creates a problem for the **administration because** there is a discrepancy between actual time worked and recorded time.
2. Will you please send me a copy of my apartment lease? When I signed it, I forgot to keep a copy for myself. I understand that I will need **it when** I apply for residency rates at school this fall. Your immediate attention is requested, and I thank you for your assistance.
3. The stories you have sent us for possible publication in our magazine are very effective. However, we do not have a need for fiction at this time. Please consider sending us some general-interest nonfiction **pieces if** you would like. Our magazine is always interested in finding talented new writers.
4. Your payment is due, Ms. **Morgan, as soon as** the bill is received. We will be forced to shut off your cable service if we do not receive a check for $82.50 by Monday. Although we value you as a **customer, we** cannot delay action any longer.
5. Travel now and receive over $200 in extra benefits. We will send you dinner certificates, discount coupons for museums, and two-for-one offers from many leading merchants in town. Unless you call **now, you** will miss out on this great offer from TravelPro.com.

## Exercise 5, page 30

1. (3) The conjunction *so* correctly shows the correct relationship between the two independent clauses.
2. (4) The subordinating conjunction *although* matches the relationship shown by *but* in the original sentence.
3. (2) The conjunction *and* shows the correct relationship.

**4.** (5) The conjunction *or* shows the correct relationship of choice in this sentence.

**5.** (3) The subordinating conjunction *since* matches the relationship indicated by *because* in the original sentence.

### Exercise 6, page 31

**1.** (4) were talking
**2.** (1) blows
**3.** (5) would have responded
**4.** (2) work

### GED Practice, page 32

**1.** (5) The coordinating conjunction *but* shows the correct relationship between the two original sentences.

**2.** (2) The original sentence uses *but* to show contrast, so the revised sentence should also show contrast. The subordinating conjunction *although* is correct.

**3.** (3) There is no contrast between the two clauses, so *although* is incorrect. The subordinating conjunction *if* shows the cause-effect relationship.

**4.** (5) The original sentence is a run-on. Choice (5) corrects this error.

**5.** (5) This sentence is correct as written.

**6.** (2) Choice (2) corrects the sentence fragment by using the appropriate subordinating conjunction *when*.

**7.** (4) The correct tense is future: *will help*.

### Cumulative GED Practice, page 34

**1.** (5) The subject of the verb is *families*, which is plural: *families have*.

**2.** (2) A comma is necessary when the dependent clause comes first in the sentence.

**3.** (5) The subject of the sentence is *benefits*, which is plural: *benefits are*.

**4.** (3) The plural form of the noun is correct, not the possessive.

**5.** (1) The verb must agree with the plural subject *children*.

**6.** (2) The plural form *educators* is correct, not the possessive.

**7.** (5) This choice corrects the run-on by creating a compound sentence.

**8.** (2) The verb should be in the past tense; the clue words are *last Thursday*.

**9.** (3) The present perfect tense of *do* is *have been doing*.

**10.** (4) The subject in this inverted sentence is *estimate*, a singular noun, so the verb is *is* correct.

**11.** (4) This sentence corrects the fragment in the original text. The correct cause/effect relationship is expressed.

**12.** (1) The indefinite pronoun everyone is singular: *everyone thinks*.

**13.** (3) The two clauses are not contrasting, so *but* is not a good conjunction to use. The conjunction *and* is the best choice.

# Organization

### Exercise 1, page 38

**1.** Yes
**2.** Yes
**3.** No
**4.** Yes
**5.** No

### Exercise 2, page 39

**1.** (1)
**2.** (4)
**3.** (3)
**4.** (2)
**5.** (5)

### Exercise 3, page 41

**1.** (3)
**2.** (3)

### Exercise 4, page 42

**1.** (5)
**2.** (3)
**3.** (4)
**4.** (4)

## Exercise 5, page 44

1. Commence to steer your motor vehicle in a southwesterly direction upon entrance to the aforesaid reservoir, keeping both hands firmly on the steering wheel of the vehicle.
2. We are making this last-ditch effort to get you to clean up your act before we call the cops and have you dragged into court.
3. Effective
4. His crabby old ma is sick as a dog and needs round-the-clock care, and Nathan is the man for the job.

## GED Practice, page 45

1. (3) This sentence about good location does not support the topic sentence.
2. (3) This sentence supports the main idea of paragraph B—what Gupta does to make his stores so successful.
3. (5) This is an effective paragraph with one main idea and several sentences that support it.
4. (2) The supporting sentences give examples of how Gupta finds and keeps good employees.

## Cumulative GED Practice, page 47

1. (5) The original sentence is a fragment. Using the command *imagine* corrects the error and makes the sentence fit with the rest of the paragraph.
2. (4) A comma is needed after the dependent clause beginning with *if*.
3. (3) The past tense *explored* is incorrect because it is not consistent with the tense of the rest of the paragraph, which is the future tense.
4. (1) The verb *offer* agrees with the plural subject *botanists*. Do not be confused by the interrupting phrase *familiar with the area*.
5. (3) Sentence 9 shows a shift from sentences about active vacationing to sentences about relaxing on vacation. These two ideas should be in separate paragraphs.
6. (3) The conjunction *but* incorrectly indicates a contrast. The conjunction *as* is a better choice to show the time relationship between the two clauses.
7. (4) A sentence about restaurants in the United States does not support the main idea of the advantages of a cruise vacation. The sentence should be removed.

8. (5) This sentence is correct as written.
9. (4) The correct possessive pronoun is *your*. Do not use the contraction *you're*, which means *you are*.
10. (2) The conjunction *but* correctly preserves the contrast of the original sentence's *although*.
11. (5) The tone of the last part of the sentence does not fit with the rest of the piece of writing. It is too casual, and it uses slang terms.
12. (3) The subject of the sentence is plural: *variations*. The verb *are* agrees with this subject.
13. (5) All sentences in paragraph C relate to keeping the mailbox clear of debris for ease of delivery.
14. (2) The original version is a run-on sentence. Choice (2) correctly divides the run-on into two separate sentences.
15. (2) The past tense *arrived* is not consistent with the present and future tenses used throughout the rest of the memo.
16. (4) The subject of the sentence is *packages*, a plural noun. Do not be confused by the interrupting phrase *that fit on the regular mail truck*.

# Using Correct Language

## Exercise 1, page 51

**Sample answers:**

1. **Suddenly,** Mr. Petersen made the announcement over the loudspeaker.
2. The pet sitter arrived at the **correct** apartment on time and ready to work.
3. Yesterday, the employees walked **directly** into the office of their manager and demanded better working conditions.
4. We look forward to offering you **excellent** service throughout the holiday season.
5. We regretted the **disgraceful** performance at last night's concert.
6. When will you be able to bring your **new** baby here so we can meet her?
7. **Secretly,** the police officer turned the corner in pursuit of the suspect.

8. The elderly man slept **soundly** on the park bench by the river.
9. That computer looks too **old** and **damaged** to be of any use to us on this project.
10. The **inexperienced** teacher looked surprised when his students showed up unprepared for class.

### Exercise 2, page 52

1. Tears streamed down the face of the old woman, upset by all of the violence.
2. The calm president-elect began his speech to the wildly cheering convention crowd.
3. Margaret found the boxes she was looking for sitting in the back of her closet.
4. Correct
5. Needing extra help for the holiday season, retail shops have been hiring hundreds of workers each day.
6. With a disgusted frown, the rude salesperson threw my sales receipt into the bag.
7. The soft music soothed the baby falling gently to sleep.
8. The computer disk with all my work saved on it fell to the floor.

### Exercise 3, page 53

1. The stores will be crowded when we shop this weekend.
2. After you have sent out your résumé, it is a good idea to follow up with a phone call.
3. If people are driving too fast on a residential road, police cars will be on the lookout.
4. The local newspaper can sometimes be helpful when you are looking for a good used car.
5. Correct
6. One must have a certified letter to be eligible for the contest.
7. Correct
8. While Jean was on a business trip, her office was cleaned out.
9. Because he was eager to start his new job, the days seemed to go by slowly.
10. The paperwork can be completed while you wait to see the doctor.

### Exercise 4, page 54

1. Next year our tournament, the Amateur Chess League Championship, will be held in Westwood.
2. The contract, a final sales agreement, will be mailed to you before the end of the week.
3. Let me introduce to you Mr. Rick Sipe, the new sports information director.
4. Mike Gomez, one of our most valuable team members, has been named Employee of the Month again.
5. Angela, my wife's sister, organized the volunteer supper program.
6. The project, a product development timeline, will be ready for presentation once these final changes are made.

### Exercise 5, page 55

1. Studies suggest that **cutting** back on red meat, **using** whole grains, and **eating** raw vegetables can reduce the risk of cancer.
2. When the weather is hot, you should **drink** lots of water, **stay** out of the sun, and **avoid** strenuous exercise.
3. **A planned agenda** and **an organized leader** are key elements for a good meeting.
4. When you are writing, do you spend more time **drafting** your piece or **revising** it?
5. When test driving a new car, **listen** for irregular sounds and **make** sure the odometer reflects the correct mileage.
6. The new assistant **was hired** on Monday, **began** work on Tuesday, and **quit** on Wednesday.
7. Your son is **capable, kind,** and **fun.**
8. To get the job done, we will have to **work** harder, **stay** later, and **help** each other.

### Exercise 6, page 56

1. In the letter the supervisors say we'll be getting bonuses in July instead of January.
2. Mr. Davis gave John the report Mr. Davis wrote.
3. Correct
4. Doctors say you can get very sick from getting bitten by a rabid dog.
5. As she walked by the elderly woman, the little girl looked up and smiled.
6. Correct
7. Sarah reviewed the plans that Tammy drew, and Tammy had to redraw them.
8. Correct

## Exercise 7, page 57

1. their   (stepsons)
2. his or her   (everyone)
3. she   (girl)
4. its   (company)
5. their   (boss and colleagues)
6. they   (volunteers)
7. we   (we)
8. her   (one)
9. his; his   (nobody)
10. their   (violinists)
11. he or she   (someone)
12. he or she   (neighbor)

## GED Practice, page 58

1. (5) A comma is needed before the appositive *our customer.*
2. (3) The original sentence contains a dangling modifier. Choice (3) uses the subject *we* so the modifier now has something to describe.
3. (2) The sentence is now parallel in structure: *marital status, income, and employment.*
4. (1) The pronoun must agree with its antecedent, *anyone,* which is singular; therefore, the plural *their* is incorrect.

## Cumulative GED Practice, page 60

1. (1) The original is correct as written.
2. (3) Choice (3) corrects the dangling modifier *Being an important right and responsibility of citizenship.*
3. (3) Commas are needed before and after the appositive, or renaming phrase.
4. (1) No comma is needed when the independent clause precedes the dependent clause in a sentence.
5. (4) This sentence is irrelevant and should be deleted from the paragraph.
6. (4) The pronoun *they* in the original sentence does not agree with the antecedent *office;* the correct pronoun is *it.*
7. (4) Sentences 13 and 14 belong with the other sentences that state voting regulations.
8. (4) The original sentence is not parallel in structure. Choice (4) corrects the error: *live and be.*

9. (4) The original sentence 3 was a fragment. Choice (4) correctly combines it with sentence 2 using correct punctuation.
10. (1) The subject of the sentence is *reasons,* a plural noun; therefore *are* is correct, not *is.*
11. (2) The noun *United States* is plural, not possessive. No apostrophe is needed.
12. (3) The original sentence contains the incorrect verb form *been.* The verb *is* is correct.
13. (4) The indefinite pronoun *this* correctly refers to its singular antecedent, *surge arrestor.*
14. (3) The verb *recommend* is in agreement with the plural subject *engineers.*
15. (5) The pronoun *his* does not agree with the antecedent. The pronoun *your* is the correct choice.

# Mechanics

## Exercise 1, page 65

1. Our new **cousin** is named Madeleine Caviness, and she was born in **China.**
2. The manager of our sales department gave a speech at the annual **meeting.**
3. Next **Sunday** is **Greg Goldsmith's** retirement party, so all his former **employees** are holding a dinner party in his honor.
4. The **spring** is usually the busiest time of the year for Betty's Thrift Shoppe.
5. Jalil and Malik are this **year's** honored **graduates** at **Roxbury High School.**
6. Did you buy that **fur** on your trip to **New York?**
7. The delegates from both **countries** arrived at the conference ready to learn from each other and negotiate fairly.
8. Her son needed to see a **doctor** immediately, yet she was turned away from **County Hospital** without any help whatsoever.
9. The refreshment committee made the decision to serve **Mexican** food at the **banquet.**
10. All **state** governments now have the right to set a speed limit of 65 miles per hour on rural interstate highways.
11. The **newspaper** quoted **Mayor Fay** as saying she was in favor of the new gun legislation.

12. The administrative assistant sends all his photocopying to **Burns Copy Company** because of its fast turnaround time.
13. Take a left onto Ash Hill **Road,** and you will see our **house** on the left-hand side of the street.
14. The autobiographer recalled that **August** was the month she found most relaxing.

## Exercise 2, page 66

**Part A**

1. too
2. weather; its
3. brakes
4. their; they're
5. through
6. passed

**Part B**

**It's** time to review the resident policy for coffee **breaks.** People have been abusing **their** privileges by not signing in or out and leaving **too** frequently. You **know** who you are. Please remember to **write** your name on the signout sheet so that supervisors know who is **where.** If we go **through** another **week** like this **past** one, we will be forced to limit breaks to specific times.

## Exercise 3, page 67

1. Benjamin **Jones, a** construction **worker, takes** dance classes in the evening.
2. My sister bought a plane **ticket and** left yesterday.
3. Until the lawyer hears from the **client, no** action will be taken.
4. Please consider giving up your **seat if** an elderly person boards the train.
5. Wishing to remain **anonymous, the** donor did not attend the ceremony.
6. **Hamburgers and** hot dogs are on the cookout menu for tomorrow.
7. **Frustration, boredom, and** irritation are all manageable emotions.
8. The customers saw the **china, and** they fell in love with it right away.
9. I would like to introduce Mary **Jo, our** event photographer.
10. The time of the **meeting is** eleven thirty in the morning.

## GED Practice, page 68

1. (2) The noun *Maryland* is a proper noun and must be capitalized.
2. (1) The correct homonym is *their,* which shows possession.
3. (4) The correct homonym is *would,* a helping verb, not *wood,* a substance that comes from a tree.
4. (4) A comma is not needed when the independent clause precedes the dependent clause in a sentence.
5. (1) A comma should be used after the introductory phrase *For example.*
6. (2) The noun *hospital* in this sentence is not a proper noun and should not be capitalized.

## Cumulative GED Practice, page 70

1. (4) The possessive form of the noun, *management's,* is the correct choice. The plural *managements* does not make sense in the original sentence.
2. (3) To be consistent with the rest of the sentence and the paragraph, the present tense *come* should be used, not the past tense *came.*
3. (1) The conjunction *even* correctly represents the contrast shown in the original sentence, and the revised sentence is punctuated correctly.
4. (3) The subject of the clause beginning with *there* is *loss,* which is singular. The verb form *is* is correct, not *are.*
5. (4) This topic sentence introduces the main idea that Sondra Bell is being promoted. All of the following sentences support this main idea.
6. (3) The original sentence 12 is actually a fragment. Answer choice (3) corrects the fragment by joining it to the previous sentence. No comma is needed because the dependent clause follows the independent clause.
7. (4) The original sentence contains a dangling modifier. Choice (4) corrects the error by adding an appropriate subject and changing the verb *seeing* to *sees.*

8. (3) This choice corrects the unparallel structure of the original sentence. Note that the three items in the series are all nouns: *me, the Personnel Department, or your immediate supervisor.*

9. (3) Items in a series must be separated by commas. A comma is needed between *mold* and *animals.*

10. (4) The possessive pronoun *your* is correct, not the contraction meaning *you are.*

11. (2) A comma is not needed when the dependent clause follows the independent clause.

12. (4) Beginning a new paragraph with sentence 12 makes sense because it introduces a new main idea about asthma zones.

13. (3) The command present-tense *take* is correct in this sentence, not the past participle *taken.*

14. (1) A sentence about heart attacks does not belong in a paragraph about asthma.

15. (3) In this sentence *clinic* is not a proper noun and should not be capitalized.

# Preparing for the GED Essay

### Exercise 1, page 75

1. False. You have 45 minutes to complete your essay.
2. False. You can answer based on your experiences.
3. True
4. False. Readers score essays by giving them an overall (holistic) score.
5. False. Only one topic is given.

### Exercise 2, page 76

**Part A**
1. Writing
2. Gathering ideas
3. Organizing
4. Revising

### Exercise 3, page 76

1. b
2. b
3. a
4. a

### Exercise 4, page 77

1. c
2. a
3. b

### Exercise 5, page 77

This idea list would probably score a 3. The ideas are specific and relevant, but the writer has only a few.

# Gathering Your Ideas

### Exercise 1, page 78

1. Topic: Characteristics of a good father
   Response: State an opinion
2. Topic: Career vs. family
   Response: Compare and contrast
3. Topic: Biggest problem facing the country
   Response: State an opinion
4. Topic: Why people procrastinate and the results of procrastination
   Response: State causes and effects
5. Topic: Benefits of an education
   Response: State causes and effects

### Exercise 2, page 80

**Sample answers:**
1. A good father should look out for the basic needs of his children, take an active role in parenting, and spend quality time with his children.
2. While my career is very important to me, it could never replace the relationship I have with my family.
3. The biggest problem facing our country today is the threat of terrorism.
4. People procrastinate because they want to put off unpleasant tasks for as long as possible.
5. An education opens the door to new opportunities.

**Exercise 3, page 81**

Go over your idea lists with another student or your instructor.

**GED Practice, page 82**

**Part A**
1. The causes and effects of new forms of communication on people's lives
2. State causes and effects
3. Go over your idea map with another student or your instructor.

**Part B**
Follow the instructions to figure out ways to gather ideas more effectively. Share your completed idea list with another student or your instructor. Ask that person to rate your idea list. How can you continue to improve?

# Organizing Your Ideas

**Exercise 1, page 84**

1. Time order
2. Comparison and contrast
3. Cause and effect
4. Order of importance
5. Comparison and contrast
6. Cause and effect
7. Time order
8. Order of importance
9. Time order
10. Order of importance

**Exercise 2, page 85**

1. Selection

> wide selection
> many choices of style

Convenience

> no refunds or exchanges
> convenient
> located in many neighborhoods
> open the same hours as
> other stores

Price

> low prices
> a complete outfit costs less
> than a new shirt
> good shoes cost $10 or less

2. Cross off: *no return on items*
3. The group on selection has only two supporting ideas. You could add specific ideas about choices of color and choices of style
4. The ideas can go in a variety of orders. Share your ordering with your instructor or another student.

**GED Practice, page 86**

Share your answers for parts A, B, and C with your instructor or another student.

# Writing Your GED Essay

**Exercise 1, page 87**

1. b
2. b
3. a
4. a
5. a

**Exercise 2, page 88**

**Part A**
a. 5
b. 3
c. 4
d. 1
e. 2

**Part B**
a. Concluding paragraph
b. Body paragraph 2
c. Body paragraph 3
d. Introduction
e. Body paragraph 1

**GED Practice page 89**

Go over your essay with your instructor or another student.

# Revising Your GED Essay

**Exercise 1, page 92**

This essay would likely receive a score of **2.** It has some detail but lacks development. The ideas seem to be limited to listing, and several ideas are irrelevant. There are also a number of errors in Edited American English, though they do not interfere with comprehension. The essay does have an identifiable organizational plan, but not all of the information is organized consistently.

**Exercise 2, page 94**

Go over your revised paragraph with another student or your instructor.

**Exercise 3, page 95**

My best friend is my dog, **Abby.** She is **loyal, cuddly, and sweet.** I love her very **much, and** I don't know what I would do without her. Last month she got very sick, so I took her to the vet. The vet said she **had** a tumor and needed an **operation.** The **operation** was very **expensive, but** I saved up enough money for it. **She** was very **weak** after her surgery, so I took special care of her. Now she is almost back to her old **self, running around the backyard and chasing birds.** I am so **relieved** that she got better.

**GED Practice, page 96**

Share your revisions with another student or your instructor.

# Review of the Writing Process

**GED Practice, page 98**

Share your essay with another student or your instructor.